ON THE
RAZOR'S
EDGE

THE STORY OF
THE ART *of* SHAVING®

ON THE
RAZOR'S
EDGE

ERIC MALKA

Advantage | Books

Published by Advantage Books, Charleston, South Carolina.
An imprint of Advantage Media.

ADVANTAGE is a registered trademark, and the Advantage colophon is a trademark of Advantage Media Group, Inc.

Printed in the United States of America.

10 9 8 7 6 5 4 3 2 1

ISBN: 979-8-89188-101-3 (Paperback)
ISBN: 979-8-89188-102-0 (eBook)

Library of Congress Control Number: 2024909560

Cover design by Analisa Smith.
Layout design by Ruthie Wood.

This publication is designed to provide accurate and authoritative information in regard to the subject matter covered. It is sold with the understanding that the publisher is not engaged in rendering legal, accounting, or other professional services. If legal advice or other expert assistance is required, the services of a competent professional person should be sought.

Advantage Books is an imprint of Advantage Media Group. Advantage Media helps busy entrepreneurs, CEOs, and leaders write and publish a book to grow their business and become the authority in their field. Advantage authors comprise an exclusive community of industry professionals, idea-makers, and thought leaders. For more information go to **advantagemedia.com**.

To my loves

Myriam, Dylan, and Brandon.

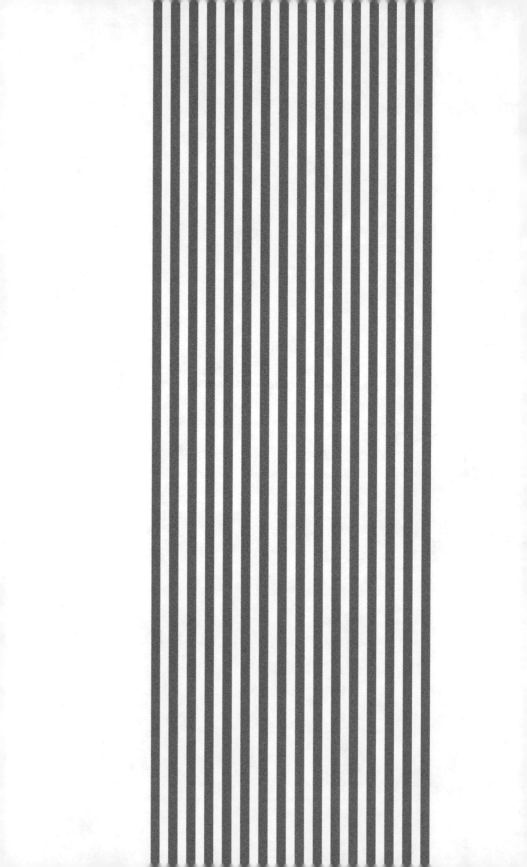

CONTENTS

INTRODUCTION

In 2009, months after selling The Art of Shaving (TAOS), I was having a casual conversation with the men's grooming president at Procter & Gamble (P&G). He shared with me that the entire P&G management team was adamantly against buying my company before the sale was made. The only two proponents in favor of the acquisition were himself and another very powerful member of senior management. Hearing this anecdote for the first time made me realize that the window to sell my company was much smaller than I had ever imagined. At that moment I realized how incredibly lucky I was to have threaded that needle in my life. A tiny difference would have caused my life to go in a very different direction.

The sheer improbability of accomplishing what I had managed in my career became profoundly clear to me. Had it not been for grit, prudence, and lots of luck, I would not have been in the position to write this book today, sharing my story and recounting all the lessons I learned along the way.

I am not a professional writer or an Ivy League professor. I am just an ordinary person who had an extraordinary entrepreneurial journey. I am one of the few entrepreneurs who built a luxury consumer brand and took it from a start-up, with humble beginnings that began at my home kitchen table, to strategic acquisition.

The business, I later learned, was simply a launching pad for the passion I would discover long after I closed the deal with P&G. After many ups and downs, I discovered what I was meant to do, and now, I am in a rewarding position to help others achieve their entrepreneurial goals as a business coach and as an angel investor. Reading this book, I hope, will inspire you to embark on your entrepreneurial journey and help you navigate your business.

CHAPTER 1

On the Razor's Edge

"It's not about the cards you are dealt, but how you play the hand."

—Randy Paulsch

I was seventeen when I arrived in NYC as an undocumented immigrant with no money and no education. Twenty-four years later, my company was acquired by a Fortune 25 corporation.

This is my story!

When I started my career, I was at a real disadvantage. I didn't have any business experience or a green card to get a job. Add to that, I was underage living in a new country, and my lack of self-confidence made it feel like my aspirations were completely out of reach.

So, with all odds against me, how did I achieve a high level of success in my career and life?

Was I fortunate? Was I so determined that failure was not an option for me? Did I have a unique talent, or was it a combination of all those elements?

It's hard to say because a single component cannot explain my success.

In fact, I now realize that some of my weaknesses turned out to be my strengths. Not having a college degree allowed me to think freely and creatively. Not having money made me hungry and more resourceful. Not having a green card bolstered my desire to become an entrepreneur. Not having a plan B made me incredibly resilient and tenacious.

There is no road map that can guide you down a direct route to becoming a successful entrepreneur. No two success stories are identical, yet they are all similar in many ways. I think of entrepreneurs as treasure hunters. Every one of us who ventures into entrepreneurship has a map called a "business plan" before embarking on our journey to find the treasure. Along the way, we find clues that lead us toward other opportunities. Sometimes, we go down the wrong path and must go backward to correct the course. At times, we encounter dangerous pitfalls that threaten our business's existence. Other times, we encounter situations and people that propel us forward toward our goal. My objective with this book is to provide you with as many clues as possible that can help you find your own treasure.

Most, if not all, entrepreneurs I meet aspire to build and sell their businesses one day and have a significant liquidity event, but only a small fraction actually achieve that goal.

According to the latest data from the US Bureau of Labor Statistics (BLS), approximately 70 percent of US private companies fail within ten years. Of the 30 percent that make it past the ten-year mark, a tiny percentage achieve a big exit, and among those that complete an exit, a handful are brands consumers are familiar with. Statistics from the US Census data show that the odds of a start-up reaching $10 million in annual sales within six years is less than 1 percent. The odds of reaching $50 million is 0.1 percent and reaching $100 million is 0.035 percent. If you aspire to build a billion-dollar company, the odds of success is 0.00006 percent.[1]

With astoundingly low success rates, what can an entrepreneur do to increase their odds of winning?

Having beaten those odds myself, I will unpack in this book some of the lessons I learned along the way to find answers to that question. After all, success leaves clues. By studying successful individuals' behaviors, strategies, and habits, you can uncover patterns and practices that contribute to success.

We all know we need four basic elements to start a business: an idea, people, funding, and execution. The better we execute these four elements, the more success we should achieve; however, that is not always the case. During my career, I've witnessed entrepreneurs struggle to keep their businesses running, and a lot of these were good businesses with a solid track record. What happened to those entrepreneurs who started well and achieved some level of success before it all went wrong?

I believe the answer to that question is counterintuitive as it is not what you do that will help you achieve success but rather what you avoid. In my experience, grit, prudence, and timing were the intangible elements that tipped the scale in my favor to beat the odds.

Angela Duckworth, a psychologist and assistant professor at the University of Pennsylvania, defines grit as "sticking with things

---

1   USA Link System, "Small Business Statistics 2022 Recap: What Is on the Small Business Failure/Success Rate," LinkedIn, March 31, 2023, https://www.linkedin.com/pulse/small-business-statistics-2022-recap-what-failuresuccess/.

over the very long term until you master them. The gritty individual approaches achievement as a marathon; his or her advantage is stamina."

Unfortunately, too many entrepreneurs get to the start of the marathon with a sprint-like mindset armed with a business plan to match.

The concept of "grit," popularized by Duckworth, is paramount. Grit transcends mere resilience; it is the fusion of unwavering passion and steadfast perseverance directed toward long-term objectives.

This quality is not about a momentary thrill in pursuit of a goal but a deep-seated, enduring commitment to a chosen path, marked by continuous, unwavering engagement. Grit embodies the ability to maintain effort and direction over extended periods despite the challenges, obstacles, or stagnation one might encounter. It's about the capacity for quick recovery from setbacks, the agility to bounce back from failures, and the resolve to keep moving forward.

Those with grit do not waver in the face of boredom or the temptation to alter course; their focus is unyielding and long term, prepared more for a marathon than a sprint. Central to grit is a growth mindset—the belief that abilities and intelligence can be cultivated through dedication, learning, and persistence.

Grit, therefore, is a crucial predictor of success, not just in business but across various life goals. It is the driving force enabling individuals to navigate through difficulties and persist over long periods to realize their aspirations. Unlike static traits like innate talent or intelligence, grit is dynamic, a quality that can be developed and honed over time.

For entrepreneurs, cultivating grit is not just advantageous; it's essential for the long and often challenging journey of achieving your dream.

The bigger your dreams are, the more you will be tested along the way. I have come to think of those tests as questions you hear internally at different stages of our journey: How much do I really want this? What am I willing to do to get what I want? How much am I willing to endure to achieve my dream?

To become a US Navy SEAL, elite soldiers are put through the worst physical and mental pain imaginable during what is known as "hell week." The Navy does this, not because it is sadistic but because they want to know which among these superhuman soldiers are the grittiest. Seventy-six percent of those who start hell week give up before the end.

While grit can be compared to resilience, prudence is more aligned with vigilance, but not to be confused with risk aversion. Sometimes used interchangeably, they actually mean two distinct concepts, especially in the context of entrepreneurship and decision-making. Risk aversion is a choice to avoid loss over making a gain if there is uncertainty involved. Risk-averse individuals are primarily concerned with minimizing risk, sometimes even at the expense of potential rewards. Therefore, risk aversion is a nonstarter to becoming an entrepreneur.

In entrepreneurial bravado, prudence is often overlooked as a cornerstone for success. This quality is characterized by wise decision-making, foresight, and careful judgment, underpinning the thoughtfulness and discernment essential in entrepreneurial actions and decisions. Prudence is more than mere caution; it is a rational assessment of situations, meticulously considering potential consequences and risks before taking action.

Prudent entrepreneurs are known for their foresight, ability to anticipate future scenarios, and adeptness at strategically planning to circumvent potential problems or seize upcoming opportunities.

Their decision-making process is marked by judiciousness—a careful and balanced consideration of all relevant factors, assessing both the benefits and drawbacks and thoughtfully weighing their decisions' short-term and long-term implications.

Self-discipline is another critical aspect of prudence, manifesting in the entrepreneur's ability to exercise control over impulses and desires, choosing actions that are rational and well considered rather than being driven by emotions or the lure of immediate gratification. This self-discipline extends to a sense of responsibility, as prudent entrepreneurs recognize and assume responsibility for their actions and their potential impact on themselves, others, and the broader environment.

Furthermore, learning from experience is integral to prudence. Entrepreneurs with this quality use their past experiences, including their mistakes, to inform and refine their decision-making process. They understand that wisdom is not just born from success but often from the lessons learned through failure.

In the realms of business, finance, and leadership, where decisions can carry significant and far-reaching consequences, prudence is not just beneficial—it's imperative. It's about striking a balance between ambition and innovation on the one hand and wisdom and careful planning on the other. Therefore, prudence emerges as a guiding light, steering the entrepreneurial ship through calm and turbulent waters.

To use a sports analogy, in tennis, the player who often wins is the one who had the least number of unforced errors during the match. The same is true in business. If entrepreneurs reduce mistakes and make better decisions to avoid early-stage pitfalls, they can dramatically increase their odds of achieving long-term success.

The one factor we cannot control is luck. When lady luck smiles at you during your journey, it can make the difference between success and unexpected levels of success. Timing was the wild card that propelled my company to achieve the unimaginable.

Looking back on my journey, I can point to many examples of how luck gave me an edge to achieve the level of success I experienced. Some people call it fate; others call it having an angel looking over you. I call it "timing," that is, "being at the right place at the right time." Whatever you call this positive thing that is out of your control is what makes the most significant difference in the level of success you can achieve.

To be clear, I am not suggesting luck was why I succeeded. I agree with the general belief that we create our luck through the first two intangibles: grit and prudence. However, I have seen very smart entrepreneurs spend their entire careers working hard with great determination, and never achieve significant success. Were they just unlucky? Did they not seize the opportunities available to them? I believe in luck because it is not guaranteed even for resilient and hardworking people.

I believe that good decision-making and seizing opportunities when they are presented to you attract luck, while poor decisions and missed opportunities lead to more problems down the road.

We must be open-minded and have faith in ourselves, while also being enormously flexible throughout our entrepreneurial journey. One of my favorite quotes from Bruce Lee is, "To be like water." The full quote is: Be like water making its way through cracks. Do not be assertive, but adjust to the object, and you shall find a way around or through it. If nothing within you stays rigid, outward things will disclose themselves. Empty your mind, be formless, shapeless, like water. "Be like water" means that you should be formless. When Lee says to be "formless," he suggests that people shouldn't allow themselves to be trapped in a certain mindset. Instead, a person should be able to adapt to specific situations, grow, and change; that's how one can adopt the qualities of water.

Being an entrepreneur is like being "on the razor's edge," where we face a very fine line between success and failure. Entrepreneurs live in a state of extreme equilibrium where outcomes can swing dramatically based on small circumstantial changes. Simply put, entrepreneurs have a narrow margin for error, which explains why so few achieve their goals against all odds.

CHAPTER 2

A Boy from Casablanca

"There are no Jews in Morocco; there are only Moroccan citizens."

—King Mohammed V of Morocco

I was born in 1967 in Casablanca, Morocco—the youngest of four children and the only boy. My parents had my three sisters when they were in their early twenties but my mother had longed for a son. She had me eight years after my youngest sister. In those days, Sephardic Jews still placed a lot of importance on having a male child. Being a good Jewish mother that she was, I became an obsession for her while I was growing up, which didn't make my relationship with my sisters any easier.

My parents' generation grew up under French colonial rule in Morocco, which led them to have a deeper connection to the European lifestyle than to the Arabic culture. We spoke only French at home, and I attended traditional French schools.

We lived in a large apartment in a five-story building. One Jewish family occupied each floor. We were all very close friends. Our parents were always together and the kids were too, and I created wonderful memories as a result. We are still in contact with each other today although we now live in different parts of the world.

When I was five my mother left me in the bath alone to go grab a towel. As soon as she left the room, I lunged for my father's safety razor sitting on the tub ledge and dragged it down my cheek. My mother returned to find me with a bloody face. It wasn't serious but to this day, you can see the small scar on my cheek. I now think it may have been a sign that "shaving" was in my future.

Life in Casablanca was very pleasant: warm weather year-round, active social life, and fresh food. We spent our weekends at Tahiti beach, a private resort on the coast of Casablanca. Each summer we traveled to Spain, France, and Switzerland by car with a ferry that connected Tangier to Malaga. Overall, I have very fond memories of my youth growing up in Morocco.

In 1956, Morocco became a sovereign country ruled by King Mohamed V. The kings of Morocco have traditionally protected the Jewish community and never persecuted us, even today. Nevertheless, Jews started feeling unwelcome and began leaving Morocco in the late 1940s when the state of Israel was created. The majority of the 250,000 Moroccan Jews left between 1956 and 1979 for fear of persecution. A similar exodus happened across Arab nations, including Tunisia, Algeria, Egypt, and Lebanon. The majority migrated to Israel, France, and Canada. Less than 2,500 Jews remain living in Morocco today.

My family left Morocco in September 1977, just before my tenth birthday.

We settled in Montreal in a predominantly Jewish neighborhood. To ease my transition to Canada my mother placed me in a Jewish Moroccan school with a couple hundred kids from our community. It didn't take me long to meet a solid group of friends. While I was experiencing turmoil in my family life, my social life made up for it by being so vibrant. There were sixty kids in my grade and most of us were really close friends. We lived near each other, went to school together, saw each other at temple on Saturdays, went out partying together on weekends, and attended sleepaway camp together. I am very grateful to have experienced life in such a warm and loving community that gave me a deep sense of belonging and cultural identity.

My first school year in class was challenging since I had to learn two new languages: English and Hebrew. In fifth and sixth grades, I was a good student, earning a few end-of-year academic excellence awards. By seventh and eighth grades, my school results started to slip. I think it was probably due to issues my family was going through at the time.

I completed my last three years of high school in a public school far from my home. At first, having classmates from many different backgrounds was a culture shock but soon I began to appreciate making friends with kids from other cultures. While high school was socially amazing, academically, I was struggling. I am not proud of my low academic achievements in high school, although I now under-stand that some people are not built for school.

Moving to a new country at the age of ten substantially impacted me. I think this kind of uprooting can affect any child and such a change is dependent on an individual's personality, previous experi-ences, and the specific circumstances of the move. In my case, I expe-rienced culture shock as I adapted to a new language, customs, and social norms. In the first two years, I felt out of place and struggled to understand and be understood by my peers. It was a scary time for me, and it felt like everyone in my family was too busy to notice. Although my mother did her best to support me, she was not equipped to provide me with adequate emotional support and encouragement to facilitate a smoother transition.

I experienced a range of emotions, including sadness, anxiety, and loneliness. I not only felt a sense of loss and grief for the familiar surroundings and routines I had left behind but also because our life in Morocco was so magical compared to Montreal.

At first, making new friends was challenging due to differences in social dynamics, school environments, and extracurricular activities that made it difficult to fit in. Within a couple of years I started adapting and even thriving both academically and socially.

While moving from one country to another presented challenges, it also had several positive effects on my development later in life. I fostered a more open-minded and tolerant worldview by being exposed to many different cultures. I developed a greater appreciation for diversity and an ability to adapt well to very different social and cultural settings.

Although Montreal is predominantly French-speaking, I grew up in an English-speaking neighborhood. At school, I was taught three languages: English, French, and Hebrew. Immersion in English led me to become bilingual and paved the way for me to learn Spanish in my early twenties. Coping with the challenges of a move started the development of my resilience and adaptability. The ability to navigate change became a valuable life skill I applied to various situations in my career and personal life.

Moving to Canada brought me closer to and immersed me in American culture through television, movies, language, and ease of travel to the United States. Adapting to this new environment required me to increase my independence and self-reliance, which helped me develop problem-solving skills and a sense of autonomy.

In my mid-teens, my father, who was an accountant for a private company, lost his job, started gambling again, and had an affair. Soon after, my parents divorced. After my father left our home, my mother struggled emotionally and financially. My sisters who were all married by then no longer lived with us. I was left to fend for myself. That is when I started thinking I needed to provide for myself. I think the experience of feeling that I couldn't count on my parents to take care of me made me decide to become a self-reliant person in this world. My mindset was, "Everyone can depend on me, but I can't depend on anyone but myself."

While I still can't pinpoint when my obsession with America started, I vividly remember thinking that Canada was too small for me to be successful. I was projecting my personal and family difficulties onto Montreal, which made me despise the place at the time. My *family* didn't have prosperity there so I believed *I* wouldn't have prosperity there. I couldn't wait to escape. Nowadays, I experience Montreal with much appreciation and fondness, although I still avoid visiting during the winter months.

I managed to graduate high school and went on to CEGEP (Collège d'enseignement général et professionnel), which is a preuniversity diploma of college studies roughly equivalent to a combination of grade twelve and the first year of an associate's degree in the United States. Reviewing my first-semester grade book showed I missed too many classes to be graded. At that moment, it became apparent that school was not the right path for me.

So, not long after I turned seventeen, I decided to quit school. For the next six months, I went out partying every night, smoked weed, and slept in late. My mother's last hope for academic success for one of her four children went up in smoke (pun intended).

A good family friend who operated shoe stores in Montreal gave me my first job. It was my introduction to the retail business. Little did I know this experience would be beneficial later in my career.

One Sunday, after an argument with my mother in a fury, I decided to leave home. I crashed at my friend's house for a week before renting a small, inexpensive apartment in the basement of a run-down apartment building. After two uncomfortable months of living alone, I returned to my mother's house.

A few months later, I left again. This time, I would not return.

CHAPTER 3

A Chip on My Shoulder

"It's never come easy for me. I don't think my mind allows me to rest ever. I have, I think, a chip on my shoulder, and some deep scars that I don't think were healed."

–Tom Brady

My "daddy issues" are deep, but I no longer hold resentment toward my father. As I matured and with the help of therapy, I began to understand he did the best he could with the tools he had. Growing up, I felt my father was disappointed in me for not being the kind of son he wanted. A son that was more like him: athletic, macho, and fist fighter tough. He just didn't have much emotional bandwidth for me. I internalized it as "my dad doesn't like me much." After years of therapy and self-improvement, I realized that those early feelings directly caused me to have low self-worth.

When my parents divorced after twenty-five years of marriage, I lost touch with my father, and we drifted apart until I was twenty-four years old.

In hindsight, unconsciously, I learned from my father what I didn't want to be in my life. I didn't want to work for someone my entire life and pour my blood, sweat, and tears into a company, only to be fired at a vulnerable age. I didn't want my children to experience financial hardship as I did growing up. I wanted to become a respected member of my community. Unlike him, I wanted a healthy and loving relationship with my spouse. Most important of all, I wanted to be a hands-on father.

In my mid-teens, when my family was faced with financial difficulties, I was at an age when I wanted to buy stuff and be like many of my friends from upper-income families. Case in point: my best friend's dad drove a Rolls-Royce! Meanwhile, I couldn't afford the latest fashions; even worse, we couldn't afford good-quality winter gear essential for the brutal Montreal winters. It was traumatizing for me to always feel very cold from head to toe when outside my house. Frankly, it was also embarrassing.

Seeing all the affluent families in my community, many self-made, gave me a front-row seat to how the other half lives. That influenced my belief that I, too, could be successful.

By the time I started college, I could barely afford the bus fare, and wasn't all that interested in school. The final blow came when my girlfriend broke up with me because her family disapproved of our relationship. *I wasn't good enough for her.*

That was, in hindsight, a perfect storm to put a chip on my shoulder and, with it, some serious fire in my belly. From that moment on, I was on a mission to succeed against all odds. Nothing would stand in my way of proving the people in my life wrong. Nothing!

I credit my need to succeed to those teenage experiences, and this need grew into an obsession that helped me develop the grit, determination, and resilience necessary to achieve a rags-to-riches success story.

On the surface, I wanted to get out of poverty, but deep down inside, I was determined to prove to the world that I was worthy.

Can you relate?

Many successful entrepreneurs don't showcase the chip on their shoulders, but if you dig deep into their past, I guarantee you will find the source of their drive, a reason why they are dead set on succeeding.

Elon Musk faced challenges during childhood. He has spoken publicly about having relationship issues with his father, who could be demanding and critical. The relationship is said to have been strained after his parents divorced. Musk also mentioned that he was bullied during his youth. Could those experiences have contributed to his drive and intensity to succeed?

Richard Branson, the founder of the Virgin Group, has often spoken about his struggles with dyslexia and his school challenges. His rebellious spirit and determination to challenge the status quo have been crucial to his entrepreneurial success.

Mark Cuban, the billionaire owner of the Dallas Mavericks and entrepreneur on the TV show *Shark Tank*, came from humble beginnings. He faced rejection and challenges early in his career, and his drive to succeed is often attributed to a determination to prove his worth.

Steven Spielberg's biography, titled *Steven Spielberg: A Biography* by Joseph McBride, delves into the filmmaker's early life and experiences, including instances of bullying and anti-Semitism during his youth. Spielberg has spoken about how he used filmmaking as escapism from the challenges he faced as a child. Creating stories and films allowed him to channel his emotions and express himself, ultimately laying the foundation for his later success in the film industry. His challenges likely contributed to his resilience and determination to overcome obstacles in pursuing his creative vision.

I am curious about what inspires people to become entrepreneurs and face the pleasures and suffering it brings. As a business coach, I often ask entrepreneurs to tell me their stories of how and why they became an entrepreneur. The details of each story I hear are different from one person to another, but between the lines, what I often hear is something that sounds like, "I needed to prove *something* to the world."

An entrepreneur I coach named Robert illustrates this point well. His little brother, John, had chronic arthritis since birth. While his family tried every possible medical route to treat his brother's condition, nothing worked. As John came of age, he started studying herbal medicine and experimenting with different natural treatments. In a short time, Robert noticed a real improvement in his brother's condition. John explained what he was doing and taking to heal himself. This caused Robert to create a company to bring this and other herbal treatments to consumers. This is a perfect example of doing well while doing good, which we will cover in later chapters. But the guilt of having a little brother with such health challenges tells me the situation may have also caused a chip on Robert's shoulder.

A "chip on the shoulder" typically refers to resentment or a perceived disadvantage that drives someone to prove themselves or achieve success. While it might not always be visible, this internal motivation can be a powerful and often overlooked driver, especially in the entrepreneurial world.

Entrepreneurs who feel they have something to prove may exhibit a strong work ethic, resilience, and determination. They often use past setbacks to fuel their ambitions, and this "chip on the shoulder" mentality can lead to increased focus, innovation, and a relentless pursuit of goals.

The desire to prove myself and overcome perceived limitations has been a powerful motivator in my career. It has also made me resilient, allowing me to bounce back from failures and setbacks, which is crucial in entrepreneurship. A chip on the shoulder can provide the resilience needed to navigate challenges and keep pushing forward.

As you will see throughout my story, I had to overcome many obstacles in my life and career. That taught me to think creatively and always find innovative solutions. As an entrepreneur with a chip on my shoulder, I was forced to think outside the box to distinguish myself from the competition.

My determination to prove myself contributed to my strong work ethic and perseverance. That in turn helped me develop a mindset and the willingness to put in the time and effort needed to achieve my goals.

The sense of having something to prove made me extremely competitive. This competitive edge was a real advantage in the very dynamic and often challenging business environment.

In his book, *Be Useful*, Arnold Schwarzenegger says if his life had been a little bit easier growing up, he doesn't think he would be writing his book today.[2] I feel the same way! My life and career would have been entirely different if my youth had been more stable. Having said that, I am aware my childhood wasn't horrible. I know many people had it much worse than I ever did.

While the chip on the shoulder was a real driver of my success, I had to balance this motivation with self-awareness and a healthy

---

2   Arnold Schwarzenegger, *Be Useful: Seven Tools for Life* (London, United Kingdom: Penguin, 2023).

mindset. Overcoming challenges was valuable, but it was equally crucial to maintain a positive mental state and avoid letting resentment or negativity hinder my personal and professional growth.

Going through therapy helped me understand how my childhood shaped who I am and brought to life what drives me. It has helped me free myself emotionally and enabled me to pursue a happy and successful life. Therapy has improved my quality of life and increased my chances of business success. We will dive deeper into this topic in later chapters.

Adversity can be our greatest ally if we can harness its powers for good.

CHAPTER 4

Coming to America

"The opportunities that America offered made the dream real, at least for a good many, but the dream itself was in large part the product of millions of plain people beginning a new life in the conviction that life could indeed be better, and each new wave of immigration rekindled that dream."

—John F. Kennedy

I am beyond grateful for the opportunities America has given me and for many immigrants like me who came to this great country seeking a better life. My story serves as a reminder to all of us that we are all immigrants and that the American dream is alive and well.

In 1985, at age seventeen, I had minimal prospects for a bright future. That summer, I decided to earn money by working in Wildwood, New Jersey, at one of the boardwalk shops that hired young boys from

Montreal. I sold my vinyl record collection to a local music shop for $100 and bought a one-way Greyhound bus ticket to NYC.

Before heading down to the Jersey Shore, I had lunch with my cousin Claude, who lived in NYC. He was a successful entrepreneur in the fashion clothing business. During our time, he explained that he had brought his younger brother from Paris to work in his company, for whom he had rented a lovely apartment in midtown Manhattan. He asked me if I was interested in coming to work for him and sharing an apartment with my cousin (his brother). I told him I appreciated the offer but had already committed to a job in New Jersey that a friend had secured for me. Years later, I learned that my mother asked my cousin for a favor to give me a job and look after me. He felt indebted to my mom for caring for him when he fell ill in her care in Morocco when he was a child.

Working in Wildwood and living with my friends in a tiny apartment was fun, but the work there did not agree with me. These boardwalk shops' business models were based on tricking tourists into spending much more money than necessary and in many cases, the customers could not afford the bill. These shops sold plain T-shirts and sweatshirts that could be customized with decals that came in hundreds of choices. The more decals we put on the item the higher the price tags. I felt this was unethical and not aligned with my values. So, I called Claude in NYC and asked him if the offer was still on the table. He said yes.

A few days later, I walked around Manhattan on a gorgeous June summer day. It was one of the happiest days of my life. I could hardly believe I lived in NYC with a job and an apartment. My dream of living in the United States was becoming a reality. I am very grateful to my cousin for giving me that opportunity.

My cousin gave me a shipping clerk position at the company's warehouse in the garment district on 36th Street and 9th Avenue. He paid for our apartment rent and provided me with a low weekly salary of $150, paid in cash since I was an illegal alien. Illegal aliens are what undocumented immigrants were called back then. I liked thinking of myself as an illegal alien, and I wore the label like a badge of honor. Illegal meant I was antiestablishment, and alien meant I was different from other humans. In reality, I was terrified of getting caught by the US Immigration and Customs Enforcement and sent back to Canada.

Each morning, I would walk up 42nd Street to Times Square, which at the time was not a very safe area; I grabbed coffee and stopped by the company showroom on Broadway to pick up the orders to be shipped that day. I would then go up to the warehouse deep in the garment district. In those days, 9th Avenue was unsafe, brimming with crack addicts and prostitutes. The smell of crack and urine was prevalent in the building's stairwells, but I didn't care. I was in heaven, living in NYC, overlooking the Hudson River from my workstation.

One morning, walking to my workplace while deep in a daydream, I stepped into the elevator of our warehouse building, and before I realized it, a man put a large knife to my throat and demanded my money and jewelry. I was wearing the bar mitzvah gold bracelet, chain, and watch that was gifted to me when I was thirteen. I had always kept my gold necklace on the tightest clip so I wouldn't lose it, which made it hard to remove while holding the day's orders in my other hand. The man became impatient with me and was waving his knife like he was going to stab me in the stomach. Terrifying as it was, I remained calm. So much so that I asked my assailant to hold my papers so I could use both hands to remove my chain. It must have relaxed him because he took the orders, and seconds later, realizing what he was doing, he threw the papers on the floor and waved the knife at me again. Luckily, I managed to unclip my chain just as the elevator door opened. He took the gold and shoved me out of the elevator. That's when my heart sank to my feet and started to pound intensely, catching up with the shock and fear of the incident.

Later in life, I experienced a similar calmness in other dangerous situations. I credit that to helping me avoid a significant car accident one day. Everything was moving slowly, allowing me to avoid a head-on collision by inches. Looking back on how calm I was in situations where most people would panic, I realized that I am wired for high-stress situations, a character attribute that would come in very handy throughout my career.

After a few months in New York City, I started feeling lonely; I missed all my friends back home. So, I called up one of my closest friends, Albert, who had also left school, and asked him if he wanted to come stay at my place for free. He arrived a week later.

Life in the city became much more fun with a wingman at my side. Soon after, my cousin also offered Albert a shipping clerk position. We were inseparable, working together to ship orders by day and partying by night. But our salaries didn't get us far in New York City. We were paid on Fridays and broke by Monday morning, surviving each week by getting credit tabs with local vendors. At our lowest point, we lived on boxed mashed potato flakes for three days straight. NYC is a tough place that can break you or help bring out the best in you. I will never forget that period as one of the most formative experiences in my life.

My younger cousin started dating a girl who soon moved in with us. Before I knew it, he asked Albert and I to move out. Homeless in NYC, we would spend each night at different crash pads, settling anywhere we could lay our head. Sometimes, we slept at the office showroom or even at the warehouse. When I was that young, situations like that didn't feel so bad. I empathize with people facing hard times later in life.

One day, while shopping for music at Tower Records, I met a girl. Her name was Donna. We started dating, and before long, I was staying at her place every night. My career prospects in NYC had already felt bleak when she asked if I wanted to relocate with her to Puerto Rico. "Where is Puerto Rico?" I asked. "In the Caribbean," she responded. "Hell, yes," I said immediately. After suffering Montreal and NY winters since my early teens, I was ready to spend every season in the tropics.

For many people, moving to another part of the world sounds impossible. It was an easy decision for me because it was an apparent choice between struggling in New York City versus living in the Caribbean with my girlfriend. Additionally, I had been taught in my youth that moving to another country or city on the other side of the world was not the end of the world.

While the transition had been challenging for me as a child, it proved to be very beneficial training for removing the fear of acclimating to different cities, countries, and even continents later in my life. My ability to relocate and pursue adventures throughout my youth was essential to my success. Throughout this book, you'll learn that after NYC and Puerto Rico, I moved to Miami, then back to New York, and then back to Miami, where I've lived for the past twenty-two years. Each of these moves brought me closer to achieving my goals. Had I not made any of those moves, my life and my career would have looked very different.

At the start of my entrepreneurial journey, I knew where I was (point A) and where I wanted to go (point B). Point B was my big vision of becoming financially successful. These big visions are a constant unless you decide to change your vision along the way. The journey, however, is entirely variable. There is no standard or set path to entrepreneurial success. The pursuit of our dreams requires extreme open-mindedness and flexibility. In my case, that journey had to go through Puerto Rico, Miami, New York, and back to Miami with all the adventures and people I met along the way, each of which brought me closer to my goals. Being extremely open-minded and flexible is critical to success. While every journey is different, in hindsight, you will see how each dot is connected to create your unique path to success. If you are heading the wrong way, pivot, try a different path, and lean forward.

Flexibility in work and life is directly related to decision-making. Each day you are going to be faced with hundreds of decisions and you'll be tempted to overthink many of them. This may be due to a lack of confidence in our judgment or sometimes due to a lack of experience. To avoid this, it is essential to use methodologies to make sound decisions by collecting data, evaluating pros and cons. The longer we debate decisions, the more we can be paralyzed about what to do. When faced with an important decision, ask yourself the following questions: Is it something I want? If this doesn't work out, what's the worst-case scenario? Is this decision helping me move in the direction of my goals? What is the risk? How do I mitigate the risk?

Moreover, breaking down decisions into smaller bites can reduce anxiety by focusing on a more minor decision. For example, in my personal life, I was conflicted about selling my home. I would go back and forth about how much I would be willing to sell it for. Where would I move after I sold it? Ultimately, I realized the only decision I had to make was whether I wanted to hire a realtor and list my home for sale. By breaking down the decision, I could focus on the next step instead of all the implications of selling my home. I decided to go for it since I had little to lose, as I could always refuse a low offer. If I got a reasonable offer, I would face the next decision. A decision I'd make at *that* time. If I accepted the offer, would I have to choose where to move to? A decision I could make at *that* time. You get the idea.

The more unknowns we bring into our choices, the more anxiety we bring to ourselves. Don't get ahead of yourself. Focus on what you can control now and let go of the outcome. It makes life easier that way and helps you make better decisions in the long run.

I remind myself to "trust the process" when faced with too much uncertainty. Trusting the process can be essential to success because it is rooted in the idea that your situation will eventually work out no matter how difficult something may seem. People need to have patience and faith in themselves before anything good happens to them, which means that you need to believe that you will eventually get to where you want to go.

To use the game of chess as an analogy, you don't win at chess by making one or two big moves. You win by making many small, good moves to position yourself for the win—action, consistency, and patience. Checkmate!

Central Park circa 1986

CHAPTER 5

Becoming an Entrepreneur

"If you look closely, most overnight successes took a long time."

—Steve Jobs

In 1988 I moved to Puerto Rico with my girlfriend so she could join her brother in running a clothing and apparel factory they inherited from their father. After we settled in, every morning, she would go to work at the factory while I enjoyed our small condo on a pristine Caribbean white sandy beach with my new best friend, Mimo. He was a cocker spaniel I had rescued, and he had a fun, loving personality. He always had a dog smile plastered to his face.

My lifestyle had improved 1,000 percent overnight, even though I had no money to support myself. I had no cousins in Puerto Rico offering me a job, and I needed a green card to find employment. So, it didn't take long for my financial situation to become very frustrating. As I mentioned earlier, I don't like to depend on others financially.

While sharing this issue with the only friend I made on the island, Gianni, he explained that I didn't need a green card to operate my own business in America and I could take profits as a foreign national to support myself. After all, that's precisely what he was doing as an Italian living in the United States. That bit of information completely blew my mind. As Plato said, "Necessity is the mother of invention," because when the need for something becomes imperative, you are forced to find ways to achieve it. Well, once again, a disadvantage in my life morphed into an opportunity. I decided to start my own business in the only industry I knew: clothing. Fortunately, my girlfriend had a factory that made clothes for various clients, including Fila, a well-known tennis apparel brand at the time. They manufactured different products for various brands, including denim jeans and fluorescent swim shorts.

Armed with fabric sample swatches, I knocked on several local retailer doors. My pitch was simple. I would ask buyers to show me their best sellers and tell them I could manufacture exact replicas for half the cost they were currently buying it for. This, in turn, would increase their profit margins while offering the item to their customers at a lower price than the name brands they sold.

Soon, I landed my first order to make kids' jeans for the largest department store on the island. When the excitement of this first order subsided, I fell flat with the realization that I didn't have the funds to finance the production. So, I returned to Gianni, a shirt importer, to ask him for a loan. I asked him to lend me $30,000 that I would pay back in ninety days with $5,000 interest. He was nuts to say yes because he trusted me unquestioningly with an unsecured loan that I could've never repaid. In hindsight, he wasn't crazy; he was extremely kind and generous and trusted me, as many people have during my career. I was very grateful to him.

Sure enough, I produced the order in my girlfriend's factory, delivered it to the customer within thirty days, collected payment within thirty days, and paid my friend $35,000 before the ninety-day deadline. Keeping my word has always been extremely important to me throughout my career and it has served me well. My word is my bond, and people have felt that all along the way. My ability to make people trust me is one of my powers and I've never broken that trust for any reason.

I used the rest of my profits to get more orders for this department store, which was selling jeans like hotcakes.

Next, I contacted the owner of a well-known local chain of surf shops. I pitched him with the same idea, except it was to make surf shorts instead of jeans. He was buying name-brand shorts for $16 and resold them for $32. I explained that I could deliver the same quality for $8, and he could resell them for $24, and best of all, I could engrave his brand name on the front of the shorts. He gave me a five hundred-unit test order on the spot. Wearing surf shorts made in fluorescent colors was fashionable at the time. I delivered five hundred units in bright yellow, green, orange, and blue quick-dry fabric. Less than a week later, he called me frantically and ecstatically, saying they had already sold all five hundred pieces. He couldn't believe it himself. He placed an order for two thousand additional units. Within six months, I could see many guys on Puerto Rico beaches wearing the surf shorts I was making for him. My little business became large enough to support a full-time production line at my girlfriend's factory, which was struggling to get enough contracts to stay in business. It was my first entrepreneurial success. I felt like I was on top of the world.

In 1990, Donna's brother, whom I was close with, announced that they could no longer make my products because they were running out of money and closing the factory. I asked him how much money he needed to stay in business. He said at least $100,000, and they'd still need to find more significant contracts, or it would only be delaying the inevitable. Coincidentally, I had befriended the only other Moroccan Jewish man living on the island who worked for a well-known apparel brand. He was sent to Puerto Rico from the Philippines to open a new factory and needed sewing machines. Knowing that our factory had hundreds of unused sewing machines, I asked my friend if he wanted to buy some. He agreed, so I brokered a deal to sell one hundred sewing machines for $125,000 for his company. This allowed my girlfriend's factory to continue operating for the time being. Instead of accepting their fate and my fate, my survival instincts went into gear. I couldn't lose my manufacturing facility, so I had no choice but to be creative and find a solution.

A few months later, on August 2, 1990, Saddam Hussein invaded Kuwait, drawing the United States into the Gulf War. During the 1980s, the US government had reduced its spending on military equipment and now found itself with depleted stocks to support its troops in the Gulf. My girlfriend's factory was an approved US government contractor for fragmentation vests and army-issued backpacks. In January 1991, the US government awarded them over $25 million in contracts. This was a huge opportunity that required all hands on deck. So, Donna's brother, the company's CEO, asked me if I was interested in joining the team as vice president. I was reluctant because I was still without a green card, and now, I would be an illegal alien vice president of a US government contractor, but I agreed because it was a fantastic opportunity. It also meant that I had to stop operating my small business. They both assured me we would consult an immigration lawyer to find a solution for me. I consulted four lawyers who all said the same thing. "You have no money, no education, and no family in the United States. Your only chance to get a green card is to find and marry a nice American girl." At twenty-three, the last thing on my mind was marriage. The height of my anxiety came when I found myself at a sensitive meeting with government officials discussing our business. All I could think about was that I might be the only illegal alien in the history of our country to be in a meeting with government officials discussing sensitive information during wartime. At the same time, they were probably wondering why I was sweating so much inside an air-conditioned office.

After that meeting, I realized I couldn't continue without legalizing my status in the United States. That's when Donna proposed that we get married. We had been dating for three years and although I cared about her, I didn't feel she was the one I wanted to be with for the rest of my life. But I knew this was my best chance to get a green card legitimately.

Soon after we were married, I received a Social Security number and a temporary green card. In those days, through marriage, you were given a three-year temporary green card before receiving a permanent green card. It took over six years since I moved to the United States before becoming a legal US resident. It was one of the most significant milestones of my life, along with becoming naturalized as a US citizen in 2002.

Between 1991 and 1993, we felt like we were on a rocket ship. We grew the business from $1 million in sales in 1990 to $12 million in 1991 to $22 million in 1992. This was a lot of money for kids in their twenties, and we were spending it like rockstars who had put out a gold album on the Billboard charts. We were having a blast and spending our nonworking days at extravagant places. New Year's Eve in Saint Barth, New York City, regularly, and first-class European trips. I remember foolishly thinking, "That's it. I made it; I'm not poor anymore."

By 1993, friction between my brother-in-law and my then-wife had grown. From my perspective, I was starting to feel disenchanted about living in Puerto Rico. I longed to return to the US mainland and start my own business.

I didn't think moving back to New York after living in the Caribbean for five years was an option. Coincidentally, I had signed up to attend a self-help seminar in Miami Beach, Florida. During my stay there, I fell in love with Miami. I thought it was a perfect compromise between Puerto Rico and New York and it was almost an equal distance between the two places. It was ideal for my next move. Donna and I quit working for the company a few months later and moved to Miami Beach together. We had about $250k in the bank, which I felt was a nice amount of money at the time to start a new life and my next business.

In Miami, I hit the ground running with the idea of selling music by mail order. I set up the business, rented an office in the Miami Design District, hired people who knew the industry, and went to market. By early 1994, I realized the business had failed miserably and that most of my accumulated money was gone. That business model needed a crucial piece: the internet, which was just in its infancy when I closed the business. By now, I had received my permanent green card just around the time when I felt my relationship with Donna was ending.

I had befriended a French waiter at a local restaurant near my office, where I had lunch almost daily. One day, he invited me to his birthday party, which was to take place at his girlfriend's house in South Beach. I didn't know this then, but a lovely young French lady would attend. Her name was Myriam. She was friends with my friend's French-Algerian girlfriend. I arrived at the party alone, knocked on the door, and Myriam opened the door to let me in.

We experienced an undeniable chemistry from the moment we met at that birthday party. Myriam caught my attention with her beautiful green eyes and long, brown curly hair. During the evening, I noticed she spoke French and wore the Star of David and Middle Eastern evil eye pendants on her neck. All that piqued my interest to start up a conversation. We were both vegan (an uncommon practice during that time), of Jewish Moroccan ancestry, and French-speaking. The synchronicity of our lives felt magnetic.

Myriam and I saw each other twice after that night, but she was only nineteen and lived in Paris, France, with her parents. A few days later, we each went back to our lives. I never thought I'd see her again, but that encounter had given me the clarity to leave my relationship with Donna. So, I rented a small apartment in South Beach to start a new chapter in my life. Again, I found myself financially broke, but I didn't appear broke since I was driving a brand-new BMW, the only thing I had taken with me from my previous relationship.

Looking back on my time in Puerto Rico, I recognize it was a vital part of my entrepreneurial journey. While most people between the ages of twenty and twenty-six are still in the student phase of their lives, I was starting my first business, honed my business skills, became a government contractor, experienced firsthand the rapid rise of a company, got married and divorced, acquired my green card, experienced living in a tropical country, learned to speak Spanish fluently, moved to Miami and met the love of my life. I consider my years in Puerto Rico equivalent to a business master's degree from the University of Hard Knox.

All our experiences, whether they seem related or not, good or bad, lead us one step closer to our dreams and aspirations. Sharpening your sword and honing your skills in your twenties prepare you for slaying the dragon later in your journey.

Being young gives us a unique opportunity to take more risks in business and life. By risk, I don't mean being reckless or putting yourself in harm's way. I am referring to taking chances, following your gut, and taking a leap of faith, like moving across the country or moving to another country entirely, to join a start-up. These are wise things to do in your twenties to gain as much experience as possible and hone your sword. Waiting until your forties or fifties to take such risks could be considered irresponsible, especially if you are supporting a family or have developed a good employment.

If I had a great job in New York City, I would not have impulsively moved to Puerto Rico with nothing concrete waiting there. If I hadn't moved to Puerto Rico, my destiny could have been very different. I don't consider what I did in my twenties risky because I had nothing to lose.

I had no plan B.

CHAPTER 6

A Girl from Paris

"Of all the gin joints, in all the towns, in all the world, she walks into mine."

—Humphrey Bogart in *Casablanca*

I met Myriam in late August 1994 while she was visiting her brother, who lived in Miami. After she returned home to Paris, we spoke a couple of times by phone. I even sent flowers to her house for her twentieth birthday. After that, I gave up on the idea that she and I would ever be together.

A few months later, she called me to announce she was traveling back to Miami to visit her brother. I was beyond excited to see her again. When I picked her up at the airport, she had a sore throat, so I took her back to my place and prepared a special herbal tea to boost her immune system and soothe her throat. I also prepared a vegan salad for lunch. She later told me she was very impressed because young Moroccan Jewish boys were not into those kinds of natural remedies. She loved that I was a modern version of our shared Moroccan Jewish culture. I liked that about her too and from the start it felt like we were perfect for each other.

We were in love, but we were young—I was twenty-six, and Myriam was only twenty. It was a matter of many months and some near misses before we became romantically involved. I was going through a divorce, and Myriam was so young that she wasn't looking to jump into a serious relationship.

We maintained a months-long, platonic friendship before allowing our feelings to guide us. We took the plunge and moved in together in South Beach—along with Myriam's brother's dog, a black shar-pei named Julian, whom she cared for.

We were an instant family.

Myriam's brother was a well-known club promoter on South Beach at the time. Myriam helped promote his parties by handing out flyers daily and working the club door by night. We spent the next six months partying together in South Beach until I maxed out my credit cards. Myriam didn't realize I was broke during that time.

I decided to get a job to support myself. I checked the wanted ads in the *Miami Times* and saw an advertisement for a financial controller at a clothing company. I was interviewed by the owner of the company at her lovely store on Ocean Drive called Island Trading Outpost. She offered me the position with a start date the following Monday morning. When I reported to work on my first day, she was sitting with a man I recognized from somewhere. After being introduced, to my surprise, I realized the man was Chris Blackwell, the famous record producer who had discovered Bob Marley, my absolute favorite artist, and U2, a rock band I love. I couldn't believe the odds of me working for one of my entrepreneurial heroes. But within three months, the company's top executives must have realized I was not employable.

One morning, I didn't show up to a scheduled call with our company's president. Instead, I was having coffee with Myriam. When I returned to the office, they fired me.

That short experience taught me a precious lesson. It demystified that someone as successful as Mr. Blackwell must have been superhuman to achieve what he did. While interacting with Mr. Blackwell, I realized he was just an average person who created something extraordinary. I told myself there was no reason I could not be as successful as him one day. For him to have discovered and produced Bob Marley and U2, he must have had many human qualities, but he also needed to be very lucky to be at the right places at the right times in his career.

Myriam picked me up after work as she often did. I informed her I had been fired and asked her point blank if she wanted to move to New York City together to find career opportunities. I think she said yes before I finished my sentence. She had always dreamed of living in the big apple. Being Parisian, she was more of a city girl than a beach bum like me.

Looking back on the past thirty years together and everything we accomplished as a couple, I understand why people say "who we choose to have as a life partner" is one of the most important decisions we will make in life. Like most love encounters, ours started with a physical attraction. Still, I later realized that attraction was just one of the many reasons I fell in love with this extraordinary person with whom I share the same values and goals. How lucky was I, and how could I have known during our courtship that Myriam would evolve to become a creative force in the beauty industry? As a self-taught product formulator, she created her first product for TAOS at the age of twenty-two. That first product, the pre-shave oil, went on to become one of TAOS's best sellers, with over one million bottles sold to date.

People often ask me how I manage working with my spouse. I won't say it was always easy, but having Myriam as my business partner has been a positive experience that produced excellent results for me, not just in building businesses but also in making a family, our home, and our lifestyle. In the early days, we butted heads, given both our strong personalities. We still butt heads, but now I know that it is healthy for us to see things very differently.

With time, we made adjustments that made working together more manageable. We drove to work separately; each had an office and separate responsibilities. We avoided discussing work issues at home or home issues at work, which can be challenging.

Choosing to have your spouse as a business partner should be for the same good reasons you would select any business partner. Choosing the right business partner is a critical decision that can drastically influence the success of your business. One factor to consider when selecting a business partner is to have shared values and vision. In our case, from the very beginning, Myriam and I realized we had similar goals and values. We didn't care much about partying, and both of us dreamed of someday starting a business. Case in point: we opened the first TAOS shop precisely two years after she moved to the United States in October 1994 and eighteen months after we moved in together.

Having complementary skills is key. Myriam is a perfect partner for me because of her incredible attention to detail and her powerful creative mind, both of which are not my strong suits. Likewise, my business acumen and strategic thinking abilities are not hers. Having separate lanes with a common goal was central to our success. Very few people master both the creative and analytical sides of the brain so it's a bonus if you find a partner who embodies the side that doesn't come natural to you.

Trust and compatibility are essential to a long-term partnership. Myriam is one of the most honest people I have ever met. As my wife, there is no one I trust more, but as a gifted professional, there is no one I trust more in their ability. Our compatibility to be business partners was also due to our understanding that I was the CEO of our business and that the final decisions rested on my shoulders. This was not because I was the man of the family but because I was the best suited for that role between the two of us. Likewise, I would challenge her ideas in her area of expertise, but ultimately, she had absolute creative control.

Myriam is a hard worker with unwavering commitment and impeccable work ethic. No matter what was happening in our personal life or relationship, I could always count on Myriam to show up and ensure her responsibilities were handled at all times.

Undoubtedly, Myriam and I achieved much more success together than we would have on separate paths.

You could say it was a match made in entrepreneurial heaven.

Myriam and Eric in NYC circa 1995

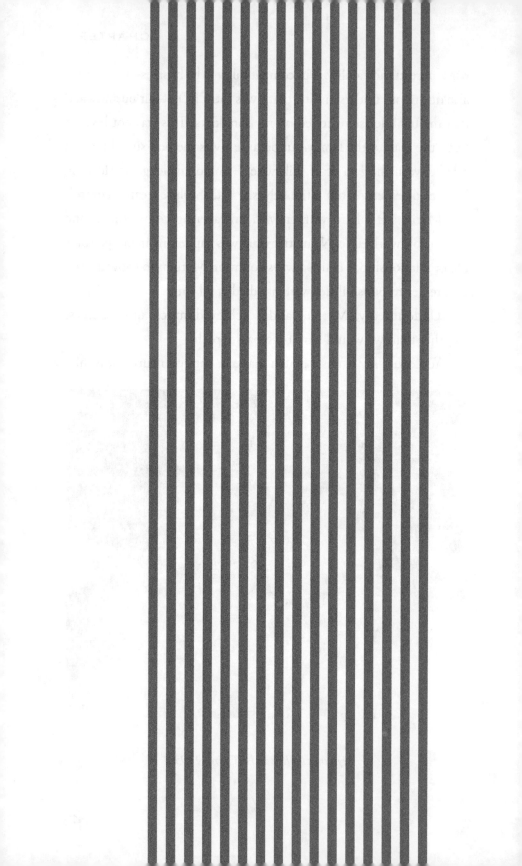

CHAPTER 7

The Big Apple

"I want to wake up in a city that never sleeps and find I'm the king of the hill, top of the heap. My little town blues, they are melting away. I'm gonna make a brand-new start of it, in old New York."

—Frank Sinatra

We loaded our luggage and our dog, Julian, in our car and made the long drive to New York City. When we drove over the Queensboro bridge with the New York City skyline in our view, music playing in the car, and our dog's head sticking out of the back seat window, it was like a scene from a romantic movie.

It was May 1995. We crashed at my sister's one-bedroom apartment on the Upper East Side for an entire month. She also helped me land a job as the financial controller for a company that sold vintage grooming products for men. Soon after starting my new job I remembered again that I was not built to work for someone else. From a young age, I had a visceral rejection of authority. I could not accept anyone as my superior. Not parents, schools, religion, or even martial arts, which I quit as soon as I was instructed to call my coach "master." But at that time, I felt I had no choice but to get a job to support us.

It didn't take long, however, for me to start feeling the itch to start another business.

While I went to work, Myriam pursued her passion for natural health by attending an herbology and Eastern medicine school. She signed up for the course to learn about natural solutions prompted by the skin issues she was experiencing. One day, as I noted my personal irritation with shaving, Myriam made me a natural, pre-shave oil that would protect my skin from the drag of the razor, based on her understanding of plant-based ingredients she was learning to formulate in school.

The following day, I told Myriam: "That was the best shave of my life."

In a burst of creativity, a new shaving brand was born. We decided to sell our car for $12,000 and use the proceeds to start the business. We brainstormed about the possibility of opening a small shop in NYC that only sells shaving products and accessories for men. We both loved the idea and agreed to start working on this new business.

A month later, with little progress made, Myriam was getting impatient about starting the business. She nagged me that I had promised to start a business, yet I wasn't doing anything about it. I responded that I was not dragging my feet; I was just too busy with my full-time job to find a store location.

The next day, I was scheduled to travel to London to negotiate terms with the principals of the leading English shaving brand my boss represented in the United States. My mind was focused on the trip, and I stopped thinking about my conversation with Myriam regarding the search for a location. But she didn't. She embarked on a mission to find us a location, focusing on Manhattan's Upper East Side, where affluent consumers live. Starting from 78th Street and Madison, she walked down to 1st Avenue, back up on 77th Street, and then back down on 76th Street. She walked for six hours until she arrived at 62nd Street between Lexington and 3rd Avenue and stumbled upon a small shop with a "For Rent" sign in the window.

Later that day, before boarding my flight back from London, I called Myriam from Heathrow Airport. I could hear the excitement in her voice.

"I found a store," she said.

"What?" I replied.

"You said we must find a store location to start the business. I found one. It's perfect. It's next to Tender Buttons, the store my aunt took me to when she visited us in NYC," she said.

Without skipping a beat, I wrote down the phone number she had seen on the shop window. I agreed to call to get more info, hung up the phone, and dialed the number. A gentleman answered and said he could show me the store that afternoon. Unfortunately, I couldn't see it that night; I responded that I was flying back from London. We agreed to meet at the store the next day. On the plane, I laughed internally, thinking this guy probably thinks I am an international financier opening a small shop for my trophy wife.

We met with the gentleman the next day and brought a beautiful catalog from the British brand we planned to sell in the store. The store was tiny and dirty, but we loved it. He agreed to lease it to us without any credit verification. I thought he believed we were a very established power couple. We later found out seven businesses had failed in that location before us. He couldn't rent this store if his life depended on it. But we were happy because the rent was within our budget, probably because of the low foot traffic on that street.

We spent over half our budget signing the lease and had about $6,000 left to fix up and furnish the store. I gave Myriam an impossible budget of $3,000 for all furniture; the rest would be used for construction and signage costs. We found a Japanese artisanal sign maker who made a beautiful hand-carved wooden sign with the store's name in gold leaf letters for $1,500. Myriam had a clear idea of the interior design of the shop. She looked everywhere in the city to find furniture for the store, but carpenters would laugh or shrug her off when they heard what our budget was.

One day, walking down 3rd Avenue, we saw a store that sold customizable wooden furniture for college students. As the store manager showed us around, we knew we had found what we had been looking for. The price of the bookshelves was within our budget, and we could customize the wood type and stain color. We ordered five bookshelves for $2,500 and used the remaining $500 to buy other pieces at the antique flea market behind our Chelsea apartment. To build and paint the space, we hired our apartment building's maintenance guys, whom I had befriended.

Lastly, we secured inventory to sell in the store from my employer. My boss, an English aristocrat turned entrepreneur, agreed to provide us with the necessary inventory on a consignment basis. This meant we would pay him after the products were sold. It was generous of him to grant this to us, which I believe he did to keep me working for his company.

Two weeks before opening day, Myriam turned to me while we were organizing the store and asked if we should start looking for a salesperson to work in the shop. Her English wasn't excellent then, and she didn't think she was cut out to be a salesperson. I told her that we couldn't afford a salesperson and that she had to be the salesperson. She didn't argue and went on to do a great job minding the store while I kept my day job. I would relieve her at the store on weekends since my job was Monday to Friday.

On Sunday, October 6, 1996, we opened for business. I was twenty-eight years old, and Myriam was twenty-four at the time. This was a monumental step toward achieving our goal.

We called the shop The Art of Shaving.

Our willingness to jump into action was always essential to our success. Even when we were not feeling ready, it was especially true when we were younger with little to lose, but we still behave this way today. If we analyze any business idea long enough, we can talk ourselves out of it. Over the years, I have learned to trust my gut and go for it.

Taking action encourages us to overcome procrastination and self-doubt and embrace the learning process of taking the first step. A leap of faith, if you will. Starting before you feel completely ready can be a beneficial thing to get comfortable with. Often, the best way to *learn* is by *doing*. By starting before you are fully prepared, you gain practical experience and learn from your mistakes, which can ultimately lead to success. Getting going can also create a sense of momentum and motivation that propels you forward. Once you begin, you are more likely to continue making progress. Many people hesitate to start because they fear failure or are waiting for the perfect moment. Starting before you're ready helps you overcome fears and build confidence while it allows you to adapt and adjust your approach as you gain more knowledge and experience. It enables you to be more flexible in response to changing circumstances. Finally, waiting for the perfect moment can lead to missed opportunities. By taking action sooner, you can seize opportunities as they arise.

Before opening our first store, we asked a few people whose opinions we respected if they thought it was a good idea. For different reasons, they all discouraged us. This taught me two crucial lessons in my life.

Firstly, I only take advice from experts with a proven track record in the subject being discussed. Some people mistake providing advice for offering an opinion. I wouldn't take medical advice from a lawyer. The same applies to people not qualified to advise on specific business matters.

Secondly, I am OK with failing as long as it means I failed at what *I thought* was the right decision. I am not OK with failing if I did what someone else told me to do.

The most incredible privilege of being a self-employed entrepreneur is the freedom to think and make decisions for ourselves.

In our pursuit of excellence in business or life, getting started is more important than perfecting it. When it's good enough … *go* … and keep making improvements. To fund our first TAOS store, we sold our car. Twelve thousand dollars doesn't get you very far in NYC, so we had to make a few compromises and break a few rules. We furnished the store with flea market antiques and local wood furniture to open our first store. Ten years later, we redesigned and refitted all our stores across the United States.

62nd Street store on opening day

Interior of 62nd Street store on opening day, October 6, 1996

CHAPTER 8

Think Big, Start Small

"Your attitude, not your aptitude, will determine your altitude."

—Zig Ziglar

Before starting TAOS, my confidence level as an entrepreneur was at an all-time low due to my prior business failure in Miami. I thought I was never going to achieve my overwhelmingly huge ambitions. I just wanted to get a job, curl up in a corner, and lick my wounds.

When Myriam and I began discussing how we were going to launch our new venture, my gut reaction was to start the business as small as possible. This was partly out of necessity because we had less than $15,000 to fund the business and because I had learned my lesson when I launched my previous business fast and furious, only to fall flat on my face.

During the first two months of operations in October and November 1996, revenues were low, but we were delighted to generate enough sales to break even. In December, our volume increased by four due to the holiday gifting season. We even had a couple of celebrities like Brooke Shields and Heidi Klum come in to buy gifts. Total monthly sales were only $37,000, but we felt we had struck gold. The store turned a nice profit. We were so excited we started discussing plans to open a second location on Madison Avenue, the most prestigious retail district in NYC. Again, we were jumping into action without overthinking about the consequences. Yes, being young and naïve can be a great asset early in your career.

Business slowed in January, but we were still motivated to open a second location. One day, a young man named Scott walked in, introduced himself as a retail broker, and asked if we were interested in finding another location. A few people did the same thing before, but we liked this guy for some reason. We said yes. We continued collaborating with this individual for the next thirty years. "What area do you want?" he asked. Without hesitation, we explained that a store on Madison Avenue between 42nd and 49th Streets would be ideal. Scott returned a few days later to inform us he had found a perfect store for us on Madison Avenue and 46th Street. Not having the necessary funds to open a new store didn't stop us from visiting the shop and agreeing to rent it. The location was on the Madison Avenue side of the Roosevelt Hotel, which was undergoing a massive renovation. We started negotiating the terms and lease even though we had no funding. Looking back, I am not sure what we were thinking. Luck would have it that the hotel manager was distracted by their renovation and dragged his feet with the leasing process of the space.

Meanwhile, I heard that Ian, the master barber of the leading British brand we carried in the shop, was coming to NYC for a shaving event at Bergdorf Goodman, where the brand was sold. I asked him if he would also do an event at our store. He graciously agreed to allocate one day for us during his visit.

Myriam and I started designing an invitation postcard to send to the four hundred customers we had captured on our mailing list. The postcard had an old-world caricature of a barber shaving a nobleman, stating, "We invite you to experience a hot towel shave by the master barber of the British prime minister and the royal family." He was the barber to Prime Minister John Major and a distant royal family member. To our amazement, we received one hundred requests for appointments. That was an astounding 25 percent return for the mailer. We asked the barber if he could add two more days to the event. He agreed.

One of our postcards got into the hands of a young French lady, who was a public relations agent. She walked into the store holding our invitation. She loved the idea of our shaving event and asked if we wanted to hire her to promote the event. I explained we could not afford a publicist. She offered to promote the event for free if we promised to hire her if the event was a success. We agreed!

In preparation for the event, we needed to find a barber chair. So, we went to local antique shops where we found a beautiful 1950s Koken white porcelain chair with a red leather seat and headrest. It was gorgeous, but the hydraulics didn't work, making the back recline flat. We bought it anyway.

On the event day, we took a broomstick to hold the chair back in the proper inclined position. This had to be done carefully and discretely between when the customer sat in the chair and when we reclined him back to start the service. Scrappy entrepreneurs have to be resourceful to make things happen in any situation.

The event was booked solid for three days. Ian, the British barber, could not have been more gracious; he was a master showman. He taught us many things about selling products as well as barbering. Each time he finished shaving a customer, the barber would sell him one of our most expensive shaving brushes and all the products needed to go along with it. We were amazed by his selling technique to offer customers the most expensive shaving brushes first. He cautioned us never to underestimate our customers' willingness to spend money on quality. A lesson I never forgot. He made me realize that the barber's credibility caused extreme customer trust, almost like a doctor prescribing medication.

The event was a huge financial success as we had our three best sales days since opening the store six months earlier. That led us to incorporate full-time barbering in our latest store location. The Madison Avenue store we were negotiating the lease for had a beautiful area in the back of the store down a few steps that was perfect for a barber setup.

The biggest win was that our publicist secured incredible press coverage for the event. CNN's Jenny Moss did a fun three-minute segment about TAOS, and *Forbes* magazine ran a full-page article. *GQ, Esquire, Men's Health,* and many others covered the event. The most significant opportunity was the *New York Times,* which requested to cover the event before anyone else ran the story. We agreed.

We eventually hired our publicist and became her first client when she started her PR agency.

With the event behind us, our focus shifted to our wedding day set for March 24, 1997. A few months earlier, I was chatting with a customer who was a well-known immigration lawyer. When I told him I was waiting for my US citizenship to be approved to sponsor Myriam's green card, he explained that we had to get married before a new law passed on April 1, 1997. In a panic, Myriam and I got a marriage license and an appointment with the mayor to be married before the deadline.

Coincidentally, the day before our wedding, on March 23, 1997, a two-page article about our tiny shop was published in the Sunday *New York Times* Metro section. Early that Sunday morning, we picked up a few copies of the newspaper and went home to read it. We were critical of how the article focused too much on the brand we carried in the store and not enough on the TAOS shop. We put the newspapers aside and continued with our day, preparing for the next morning. We had no idea about the power of the *New York Times* in those days.

I promised Myriam that, in the future, when we can afford it, we will have a lovely wedding celebration. For now, I proposed to close the store that Monday to celebrate our wedding day. Myriam refused because we had committed to having the store open from Monday to Saturday, 10:00 a.m. to 6:00 p.m., even on our wedding day. I appreciated and respected her disciplined commitment to the business. We agreed to have a few friends come to the store to have some cake after the wedding.

Early the following day, Myriam and I were married in a simple but romantic setting at the mayor's office. We took a few pictures and rushed back to open the store. We turned the corner to 62nd Street and noticed half a dozen men waiting outside the store. Strange, we thought. I heard the phone ring as I rolled up the gate and unlocked the front door. The six men walked in with us while I rushed to answer the phone. A man from Dallas wanted to mail order products he had read about in the *New York Times*. I heard the click of a call waiting and asked the customer to hold while I answered the other line. A man from Los Angeles also wanted to order the products mentioned in the article.

Meanwhile, Myriam was helping multiple customers at the same time. In a frenzy, we asked our friends to leave, and for the next eight hours, we did not stop attending to customers and taking phone orders (that's right, there was no internet back then). When the rush died around 6:00 p.m., Myriam and I looked at each other in sheer disbelief about what had just unfolded on our wedding day. The store shelves were almost emptied, to the point that it looked like we had been robbed. I calculated the day's sales; they were higher than those of the previous thirty days combined. That evening, I rushed to our supplier's warehouse to pick up products to fill the store's shelves again. The next day, we experienced the same frenzy of customers. The day after too. It went on for months.

My boss was also in disbelief, supplying us with all the products we sold at the store. When he did the quick math in his head, he realized that our little store would produce in a year more revenue than his entire company was doing after ten years in business. He invited me to dinner and, in a very diplomatic British way, explained that if I didn't make him an equal partner in our business, he would stop supplying us with products. I was shocked to hear that but didn't show it. I told him I liked the idea in spirit but had to think about it and discuss it with my partner.

We were facing the first real threat to our business and livelihood.

As I walked home that evening, I decided I had to find other vendors to supply us so that we would never have to depend on him or any one vendor again. From my travels to London, I knew that at least three other brands resembled and competed with the one we were selling in our store.

I went home and informed Myriam what had just happened and my plan. She agreed. To buy time, I started negotiating the terms of our partnership with my boss. Meanwhile, I started making alternative arrangements with new vendors across Europe.

High sales continued to pour in during April, May, and June 1997, allowing us to accumulate enough cash to fund our second location on Madison Avenue. We knew we needed all new products and vendors in place before the opening of our new store. I traveled to London and met with two direct competitors of the brand we were trying to replace. Their products looked oddly similar except for the brand name on the jars and boxes. Turns out, the same factory was manufacturing all the Mayfair London shaving brands. The competitor brands were more than willing to work with us, given our incredible volume for the category. They even gave me distributor prices that allowed us higher margins than my employer gave us.

Next, I attended a trade show in Frankfurt, Germany, where I met with a shaving brush manufacturer. The brushes looked identical to the ones we were selling with acrylic bases in ivory or black colors and they could print our brand name or logo on the front of the brushes. I placed a small order for $1,000. Myriam designed a logo for the private label shaving brushes. Ten years later, we would become that German supplier's largest client, accounting for more than 40 percent of their business. It has always been important to me to have strong relationships with our vendors. This is vital to long-term success.

By the end of June, we were ready to transition our 62nd Street store and add all the new brands we had curated. On a Friday evening, I met with my employer to inform him I was resigning from my position with his company and that the partnership deal was off the table. To say he was surprised would be an understatement. Now, I could dedicate all my energy to scaling TAOS business.

Myriam and I went to the store together the next day, determined. After closing, we removed all the old brands from the shelves and replaced them with all the new merchandise we had received. We worked tirelessly to have the store ready on Monday morning. At that moment, Myriam and I promised each other that we would never again depend on someone else for our livelihood. We committed to creating our own brand as soon as we had enough money.

We were nervous because we knew our customers were loyal to the brand we used to sell, and now, they would walk in to find all new merchandise. Regardless, we decided to be honest with our customers about our product change. The next day, some of our regular customers didn't even notice we had switched brands. When a customer did request the old brand we offered them the inventory that was left over. If we didn't have the product, we would say, "We no longer carry this brand in our store, but you can find it at Bergdorf Goodman." New customers shopped like nothing had ever happened. We lost about 20 percent of our business due to the transition of brands, but it didn't take long for us to make up for it with new customers.

Meanwhile, I worked hard building our new Madison Avenue store. We had enough money to open a store only if we cut corners and broke a few rules.

Recently, after taking a personality test, I was told that rules are just suggestions to me. It rang very true. I pride myself, like many entrepreneurs, in breaking all the rules to get what I want, but I never, ever, *ever* break laws.

When we took over the Madison Avenue store, it had moldy green carpet throughout. When we pulled off the rug, we unveiled a beautiful original wood floor dating back to the 1940s. Wooden floors would become a design staple in all our stores going forward.

I was concerned about our ability to find great barbers to work in our new shop. We contacted a barber school in our area and told them about our unique business model. Back then, high-end barber shops were less typical than they are today. Barber shops were generally low-end establishments that charged $8 for a haircut and $12 for a shave.

A few days later, the head of the barber school called to say she had a barber who had recently moved to New York from Uzbekistan. I arranged to meet him for an interview at the 62nd Street shop location after closing. When a tall gentleman came into the store at 6:00 p.m., we thought he was a customer but he was there for the barber's interview the school had set up. His name was Boris. He was shy and soft-spoken with a hefty Eastern European accent. During the interview, I asked him to perform a straight razor shave on me. I pulled one of the straight razors out of our display cases, handed it to him, and asked Myriam to carefully put the broomstick under the barber chair as I leaned backward. In hindsight, this was a desperate and potentially life-threatening move, given I never met that man before. Using some of our shaving cream and a bowl of cold water, he gave me one of the worst straight razor shaves I had ever had.

Nevertheless, I hired him for fear of never finding someone better. We trained him, and Boris became a great barber and the face of TAOS barbers in many articles about our company. He was our first hire and one of our most loyal employees for the next sixteen years. Over the years, we hired his brother, cousin, son, and daughter to work for our company. His daughter now owns and operates a successful barber shop in midtown Manhattan, which is a reincarnation of TAOS stores.

Myriam's background in the spa industry and her studies in aromatherapy and herbology gave her the tools to design an innovative menu that combined traditional barber services with modern spa techniques and products. We called it the "Gentleman Barber Spa" and we offered services such as the royal shave, a traditional hot towel shave followed by a soothing skin treatment with a mask prepared in front of the customer from fresh ingredients Myriam had formulated.

I was starting to realize Myriam had natural talents, and I hadn't seen anything yet!

The Madison Avenue shop opened in August 1997, only ten months after opening our first store. This flagship store was much bigger than the first one and now featured all the new brands and a barber area in the back of the shop. The first morning we opened the new store, I couldn't believe the hordes of men in suits walking from Grand Central Station in front of our store to get to their offices all over midtown Manhattan. Eighty percent of them looked like our target audience. The store was an instant success and became one of our top producers as we grew our company.

When we chose this Madison Avenue location, we didn't realize Conde Nast's world headquarters was across the street from the store. Every day, writers and editors of some of the most important publications in the world were walking in front of our stores and popping in to investigate. Public relations became a huge driver for our brand, with more than five thousand articles written about us during the next ten years.

In the unpredictable world of entrepreneurship, success often seems like a blend of preparation, opportunity, and a dash of luck. Reflecting on my journey, the unforeseen events propelling my business to new heights stand out vividly.

Finding a prime location on Madison Avenue at a below-market price, stumbling upon pristine wood floors that significantly slashed our build-out costs, and the unexpected explosion of our business thanks to the *New York Times* article that helped us secure last-minute funding for our flagship store—all seeming strokes of luck.

Yet, upon closer inspection, it can be argued that our actions were pivotal in influencing these lucky outcomes. This begs the question: How can entrepreneurs deliberately increase the odds of creating luck in their path?

For one, success favors the prepared. Luck will not find you. You need to find luck. Just by taking the first steps of starting your business, you put the wheels of fortune in motion. Being prepared positions you to seize opportunities and turn them into game-changing moments.

We set the wheel in motion by asking our British barber to do an event in our store, causing a domino effect. But the barber didn't just say yes randomly; I had cultivated a relationship with him during my travels to London. By networking and relationship-building, I began to understand the significance of a strong support network in exposing entrepreneurs to valuable opportunities. I was also able to gain insights into cultivating meaningful connections that can open doors to collaborations, partnerships, and unforeseen prospects.

Understanding the concept of adaptability as a secret weapon in an entrepreneur's arsenal is critical. Learn to navigate uncertainties, stay open-minded, and discover how flexibility in your approach can uncover opportunities others might overlook.

A positive mindset is critical to entrepreneurial success. Learn to maintain optimism in the face of challenges and focus on solutions rather than problems. We could have thought pessimistically about the same situation. *The barber will never want to do an event in our tiny store! We don't have a barber chair that works, and our store is too small to hold an event! We don't have to open the store today; it's our wedding day!* Discover how a positive outlook can influence your perception of events and attract positive outcomes.

You can't control luck, but you can aim for good timing in life and business. You recognize and seize opportunities by developing the awareness, intuition, and proactive mindset needed to capitalize on moments that align with your entrepreneurial goals. Uncover the strategies for turning potential into reality.

Creating your luck in the unpredictable entrepreneurship journey is not just a matter of chance or prayer—it's a strategic and intentional pursuit. By combining preparation, adaptability, a positive mindset, and strategic decision-making, entrepreneurs can increase the likelihood of experiencing fortuitous outcomes in their ventures. If you are fortunate enough to have lady luck smile at you, it can make the difference between having some business success versus experiencing extraordinary success.

For several compelling reasons, thinking big and starting small is a wise approach for entrepreneurs. Starting small allows entrepreneurs to test their ideas in a controlled environment, minimizing large-scale endeavors and financial and operational risks. By taking incremental steps, entrepreneurs can identify and address challenges early on, reducing the potential for significant losses.

A small-scale start provides a valuable learning curve. Entrepreneurs can gather insights, assess market responses, and adapt their strategies before committing to more significant investments. It allows them to refine their products or services based on customer feedback, enhancing their offerings over time.

The business landscape is dynamic and unpredictable. Starting small fosters agility, allowing entrepreneurs to pivot and adjust their approaches to changing market conditions, customer preferences, or unforeseen challenges.

When we started we had very limited resources, both financial and human. This forced us to have a lean and focused operation, emphasizing efficiency and effectiveness. In hindsight, having no resources was a blessing that I now preach to all entrepreneurs starting out.

But starting small does not mean thinking small. On the contrary, thinking big from the onset provides a visionary goal that your business idea can change the world and be an innovative leader in your industry, while starting small builds a solid foundation for sustainable growth. Starting small allowed us to validate our business idea and prove the concept's feasibility in the real world before expanding. This proof of concept is a critical foundation to ensure long-term success, attracting investors, partners, and customers as the business progresses.

Being an entrepreneur can be very demanding, both mentally and physically. Starting small eases the risk of burnout by initially allowing entrepreneurs to have a more manageable workload. As the venture gains traction, the team can scale up operations sustainably. It was not until we started building our second location that we hired our first employee.

A phased approach builds confidence. Entrepreneurs who start small and achieve success in the early stages are more likely to approach scaling with confidence and a deeper understanding of what works for their specific business model. There is plenty of time to accelerate your growth at warp speed later in the journey. If I had more resources or investors early on I may have made the mistake to move more aggressively. Scaling a business prematurely can cause significant challenges and potential pitfalls, such as running out of cash, unaddressed product quality issues, and overwhelmed operations to name a few.

Essentially, thinking big and starting small is a pragmatic and strategic approach that balances ambitious vision with prudent execution. It empowers entrepreneurs to navigate the complexities of business with resilience, adaptability, and a higher likelihood of long-term success.

Patience in the early years of a business is critical. But patience doesn't mean passivity. On the contrary, patience can require tremendous self-control for ambitious entrepreneurs with big aspirations that tend to shoot from the hip.

So, dream big and start small, my friends!

With two successful stores in NYC providing almost $1 million in profit annually, we decided it was time to develop our branded product line.

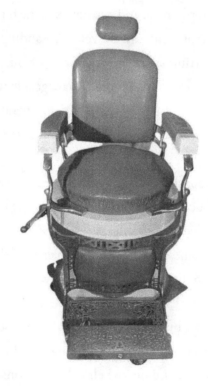

Koken 1950s barber chair

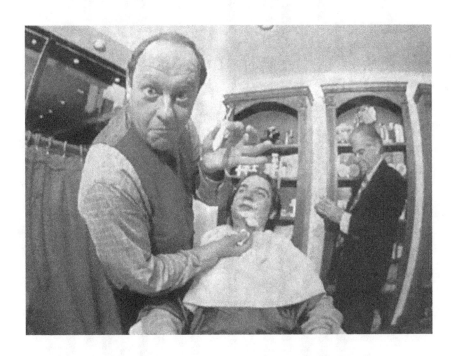

The British barber shaving me for Forbes magazine

The metal plaque outside our Madison Avenue store

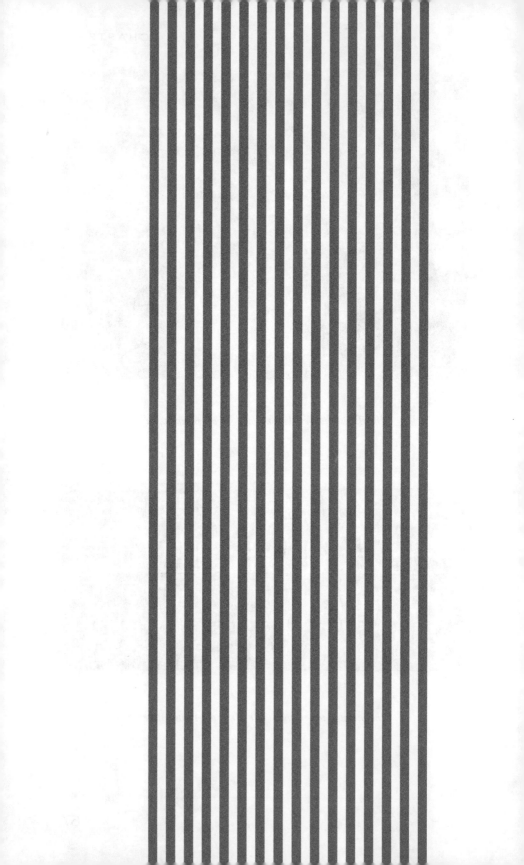

CHAPTER 9

Brand Building

"If I asked people what they want, they would have said faster horses."

—Henry Ford

During our first two years in operations, Myriam and I worked exclusively in the stores, developing the business while helping customers. This allowed us to personally listen to hundreds of customers' wants and needs. We were essentially having our own private consumer focus group, which is a brand builder's dream.

Even more astonishing, most of our customers had the same two requests. They wanted to know if we had any fragrance-free products and products for sensitive skin. Unfortunately our answer to the first question was no since every product we carried was scented. When they asked the second question, we shared our expertise on the topic of skin sensitivity. Most men have a sensitivity to the skin from the drag of the razor caused by a lack of protection from the shaving creams they use.

That critical consumer insight became the foundation for building the TAOS brand and product philosophy. All formulas we created were made with botanical ingredients and pure essential oils to be fragrance-free. Understanding that men wanted a close shave that would not result in razor burns, we designed our shaving system to protect the skin with pre-shave oil, soften the beard with hot water and rich lather shaving cream, and soothe the skin with aftershave balm or gel.

So, when Myriam and I set out to create our products, we made sure to take the consumers' concerns into consideration. For this reason, we marketed the first three products we launched as "fragrance-free for sensitive skin to soften the beard and protect the skin for a close and comfortable shave."

I had doubts that the TAOS brand could transition from store insignia to consumer-packaged goods. The brand name sounded too gimmicky for a line of products. In the spirit of thinking big and starting small, we decided to run a pilot test in our stores with three products.

Myriam would give me design direction while I did my best to create our product labels on my home computer. In the beginning we didn't have money to hire a lab to create our own custom formulas, so we had to be resourceful. We contacted the best shaving cream manufacturer in England, which made creams for many brands. We asked them if they could make a small batch of their shaving cream for us without adding colorants or perfume. Although our request surprised them, they agreed to do it, as it was an easy change. The shaving cream formula became fairly natural after removing these offending ingredients. We bought one hundred kilos of shaving creams and had them filled locally in New York. We packaged them in beautiful black jars from Italy with an old-fashioned ivory label in front.

Next Myriam contacted a chemist we had recently met who made spa products with natural ingredients. She was impressed with one of the hydrating gels he made because it was nongreasy and all natural. These chemists were rare at that time. We asked him if we could remove the fragrance and fill them in our masculine glass bottles instead. He agreed.

Finally, to reproduce the pre-shave oil that Myriam created, which prompted the start of the business, we purchased the five raw ingredients, and had them blended and filled locally. The final oil formula was packaged in beautiful apothecary green glass bottles from France, which Myriam had sourced at a Javits Center packaging trade show.

We proudly launched our three new products in our stores: a pre-shave oil, a shaving cream, and an aftershave gel. Now, each time a customer walked in and asked if we had fragrance-free shaving products for sensitive skin, the answer was, "Yes, of course." Our three self-branded products immediately became the top three sellers in our company out of the one hundred products we sold.

This was the confirmation I needed to invest in launching our fully branded line of products. It was time to really start thinking big.

Myriam was a very early pioneer of green chemistry. So, when we began to create a complete line of shaving products, we knew we wanted the brand to be based on our philosophy of natural ingredients. Looking back at the formula she created and the philosophy she developed in the 1990s, she was clearly ahead of the times. She was already pushing for purity in her formulas and promoting our ingredients' blackout list at a time when the idea of clean beauty was not even a topic of conversation. Now, all those innovations are the norm in the clean segment of the beauty industry. From the start,

Myriam had selected the highest-quality plant-based ingredients and 100 percent pure essential oils to create a comprehensive range of natural shaving products.

We needed a wide range of products to fill an entire store with our brand. So, we decided to launch twenty products at once: a pre-shave oil, a shaving cream in two sizes, an aftershave gel, and an aftershave balm, all of which came in four distinct essential oils for different skin types. We added an alum block to help combat nicks and cuts, and a selection of razors and shaving brushes. Having a complete line of shaving products positioned us as a leader in the premium shaving category. We didn't plan for that, and it became one of the most critical competitive elements of the TAOS brand.

Myriam worked closely with various labs that helped her create each formula, but it soon became evident that her philosophy was ahead of the times. In the mid-1990s, clean beauty didn't exist yet, and labs were not on board with that philosophy. We had to push them for purity and natural ingredients to the maximum extent available. But even then, our products ranged from 96 to 100 percent plant-based ingredients.

Branding our products was critical to our success, and Myriam made it her mission to identify ideal bottles and jars for each product category.

It didn't take me long to realize that Myriam was gifted in product development.

We hired a seasoned logo and packaging designer willing to work on our project as a freelancer while keeping her day job at a big design firm. She was the perfect person for the job and partner for Myriam's creative direction. She collaborated with us on various projects for the next twenty years and originally came up with the idea of the ivory backdrop of our logo in a rectangular box. We loved the idea, but something was off. Myriam and I asked her to play around with the encasing and to make it oval instead of a rectangle. When we saw the revised logo, we knew we had just created something iconic.

During this time, Myriam and I were immersed in the world of brand building. One of the things we learned was that consumers should recognize your brand just by its packaging, without the brand name. Since our customers were more traditional professional types that wore pinstripe suits and striped shirts, we thought of making our outer boxes in pinstripes. Myriam and our designer landed on the perfect tone-on-tone stripes that became iconic for the brand. The stripes and the masculine color palettes of ivory, black, gray, blue, burgundy, and yellow became synonymous with the TAOS brand. While it was beneficial to have a brand that looked like our customers, we also wanted it to be easy for them, so we color-coded the essential oil aromas because we noticed that many customers returning for refills didn't remember the name of the aroma they purchased before. We did this by providing visual cues in a beautiful array of colors that were both attention grabbing and memorable.

Consumer insight is a critical foundation for both brand and product philosophy. Understanding consumers' needs, preferences, behaviors, and desires provides invaluable information that can shape how a brand develops and positions itself in the market. This same insight helps identify the target audience's specific needs and pain points. The pain point of our customers was a choice between a close shave and a comfortable shave. We designed a shaving system that provided *both* to achieve *The Perfect Shave*. By listening to the customers that came into our stores, we were able to understand our target audience's needs early on. From that information, a brand can create products and services that genuinely cater to the consumer, establishing a solid foundation for its philosophy.

We built an authentic brand right from the start by demonstrating a deep understanding of our consumers through these insights. Consumers appreciate brands that resonate with their values and lifestyles. Authenticity, in turn, builds trust and loyalty. This is where art met science for us. We elevated the shaving category to a luxury experience that reflected our specific customer's lifestyle.

Until we came onto the scene, low-income and high-income consumers bought and used the same shaving products from mass-market retailers. This was an anomaly! In most consumer categories, from homes and cars to restaurants and clothing, there is a premium offering for premium consumers. But there was an untapped market when it came to shaving, which was mind-boggling to me because most men shave, and no one had thought of offering a premium option to affluent consumers in this category.

The awareness that our customers brought to us was priceless, and they guided Myriam in product development by providing information on the most important features or improvements to consumers. This ensured the products aligned with consumer expectations while staying relevant in the market. It also helped us identify unique selling propositions and differentiators. Some customers enjoyed scented shaving products and others wanted fragrance-free, so we delivered that in our formulas. Unscented or scented with pure natural essential oils of sandalwood, lavender, and lemon. By understanding what made our target audience tick, TAOS positioned itself effectively against competitors to stand out in the industry.

Knowing the target audience's language, preferences, and communication channels allowed us to create compelling marketing messages to ensure the brand's philosophy was effectively communicated to consumers. This one took more time. It wasn't until 2004 that we truly nailed our messaging, which I will discuss in more detail later in the book.

Consumer insight is not just about gathering data; it's about using that information to inform and shape every aspect of a brand's identity and product offerings. Like the combination of a safe, a brand must have the correct pricing, packaging, benefits, and messaging to open with ease.

In July 1998, while we were still developing the product line, the phone rang at the Madison store. A gentleman introduced himself as the operations manager for Neiman Marcus. He explained that he saw an article about our company in the American Airlines magazine and he shared that Neiman Marcus wanted to open a barbershop in its downtown Dallas flagship store. He asked if we would like to travel to Dallas to discuss the opportunity. I tried hiding my excitement when I said yes, of course. Two weeks later, Myriam and I flew to Dallas, Texas, on one of the hottest days on record. I was excited to meet with Neiman Marcus as it was a huge opportunity. Myriam was also enthusiastic about the opportunity because she was a big fan of the *Dallas* television show.

Before our meeting, Myriam bought a beautiful dress and hat to resemble a character from the *Dallas* TV show. I was a little nervous because we didn't have the brand ready to show. We were near the end of our design development phase before going into final production. Instead, I had color printouts, unbranded packaging with products inside, and shaving accessories.

We sat in a conference room with three Neiman Marcus executives—the operations manager who had contacted me, his boss, and, to our surprise, the CEO of Neiman Marcus. For the next thirty minutes, I pitched the TAOS concept to a very attentive audience. There was silence in the room when I finished, until the CEO turned to his team and said, "You guys probably don't know this about me, but my grandfather was a barber." *Cha-ching*, the sound of a cash register rang in my head. I knew I had secured a significant deal for our tiny company. We could hardly believe we had just made a deal to have a TAOS store inside Neiman Marcus.

This was big! We were stoked!

The TAOS line of products launched in 1998 and the following philosophy was printed on the first page of our catalog:

The Art of Shaving products are aromatherapy-based and specifically blended for various skin types. They are formulated with botanical ingredients and 100 percent pure essential oils individually selected for their therapeutic properties. All our products, which are free of dyes, alcohol, and synthetic fragrances, are ideal to achieve the perfect shave and to maintain, treat, and nourish the most sensitive skin.

Our branded products represented only 20 percent of our store offerings but quickly represented 80 percent of our sales. Our gross margins exploded to 85 percent, allowing us to scale our retail footprint and resell our products to retailers at a wholesale margin.

The launch of our products transformed our company from being a multibrand retailer to a luxury-branded consumer-packaged goods company.

It was a gigantic game changer!

CHAPTER 10

Crawl, Walk, Run, Fly

"If you can't fly then run, if you can't run then walk, if you can't walk then crawl, but whatever you do you have to keep moving forward."

—Martin Luther King, Jr.

I use the Crawl, Walk, Run, Fly methodology in all my businesses nowadays. It is focused on the prudent evolution of a team that thinks big and starts small. This encourages us to start slowly and speed up as we build momentum.

To use a spacecraft as an analogy, it took thirteen years to build the Apollo 11 spacecraft, but it only took four days, six hours, and forty-five minutes to fly from Earth to the moon. Had NASA engineers precipitated the stages before "launching the rocket," history may have been very different.

The discipline to move slowly in the early stages will pay off in warp speed when you are ready to add rocket fuel to your company and take off. Crawl, Walk, Run, and Fly is based on the natural human progression from birth to adulthood. There are four stages a business goes through in its life cycle, from start-up to exponential growth stage.

As I reflect on the evolution of TAOS from start to exit, I realize we instinctively went through the same four stages. Could this be one of the reasons our company was successful? It took ten years for our revenue to grow from zero to $14 million. Then we started flying, growing from $14 million to $30 million in two years. We reached $50 million three years later, and three years after that, we reached $100 million. This type of growth is called a Hockey Stick Exponential Growth Curve or a J curve. (*See the chart.*)

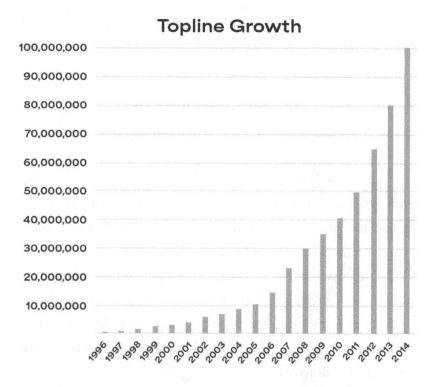

Topline Growth

Entrepreneurs can maximize their chances of success by following the natural evolution of a company or project. The order and succession of these stages must be respected, but the time a company stays in each stage can vary significantly from one company to another. Skipping any of these stages can be detrimental or even fatal to an entrepreneur. Trust me, I know from experience.

The crawl stage for start-ups includes creating a business plan, setting up the business, finding people, and developing the identity and products or services.

The walking stage consists of going to market, validating the business model, identifying the target audience, confirming the market fit of your product or services, and even going back to the crawling stage to adjust your product or business strategy as necessary.

The run stage starts once you have confirmed your business model is working. It is now time to scale your business. As you start picking up momentum, decide if you want to grow organically (continue running steady) or exponentially (start flying). If the decision is to fly, the entrepreneur or business may require raising capital (rocket fuel) to launch the business to the moon. Funding is usually necessary for this stage, as companies that grow exponentially tend to operate at a loss during that period.

The fly stage starts once you have a strong foundation, the management team in place, processes in line, and enough funding to grow your business exponentially in an almost vertical ascent.

I use this process to assess companies I invest in, and for entrepreneurs I coach. Recently, a young entrepreneur pitched me to invest $1 million in his business. I loved his vision; however, when we started our due diligence on the business, we found that he had skipped the walk and run stages and had gone straight to flying. He was now raising funds to sustain heavy losses caused by a poorly run operation.

This business operated seven unprofitable company-owned stores due to meager revenues per store.

Meanwhile, he had brought in a team to help franchise his concept. He had sold twenty franchises when I met him. His franchise company was losing even more money than his retail operation. Instead of investing, I started advising him on how to get the business back on track before it was too late. I recommended he take a few steps back to strengthen the company's business model before returning to franchising. Essentially, I was telling him to slow down and return to the walk stage.

The first thing we did was to cut his franchise company expenses by $500,000. Then, we refocused his attention on getting his stores to profitability. When we looked at each store's profit and loss statement, we noticed that three of the seven stores accounted for 80 percent of his losses. Closing those stores and focusing on the remaining four would increase his chances of reaching profitability faster. He may not need to raise funds to grow the franchise business when his stores are profitable. Or he might raise funds at a higher business valuation, resulting in less equity dilution.

In another recent case, I coached an entrepreneur whose business was negatively impacted by the pandemic. His sales had dropped by 65 percent when he was pushing the business to exponential growth. Unfortunately, he did not react fast enough to reduce costs, resulting in a severe cash flow crunch. His strategy was to scale the revenues to stop the frantic bleeding. That strategy rarely works. An analogy is like first responders trying to do physical therapy on a wounded person at the scene of an accident. First, you try to stabilize the patient and stop the bleeding. Then, you start the process of rehabilitation. Entrepreneurs caught off guard by a crisis often do too little too late to save the business. Within three months of coaching, this entrepreneur was able to reduce his costs by $1.5 million per year without hurting the business. When he starts growing his revenue again, it will be for a much more efficiently run company, resulting in high profitability. More on crisis management later in this book.

In the early days, Myriam and I crawled to get our company off the ground by selling our car and hustling to open a tiny store. We then walked when we started building enough momentum in our first shop to fund the opening of a flagship store on Madison Avenue and develop our own branded line of products.

In 1999, it was time to start running. That year, we opened two new store locations. One was on Wall Street, and one was on the men's floor of the Neiman Marcus downtown Dallas flagship store. Given the number of professional men working in that area, we thought the Wall Street store was a no-brainer. Unfortunately, the store was off to a slow start, which proved to be a new challenge we had not faced with our first two successful stores. It didn't take us long to determine the issue. The store did almost no business on Saturdays and Sundays since financial markets are closed on weekends, and weekends accounted for 40 percent of our gross sales. We learned an important lesson for future real estate location decisions.

The Neiman Marcus shop didn't do very well either since it was on a low-traffic floor in a low-traffic store. This caused us to stop running and return to the walking stage to fine-tune our business model. Wall Street taught us the three most important rules in retail: location, location, and location.

Although the Dallas shop was a small producer, it allowed TAOS to start a relationship with Neiman Marcus. It also gave us bragging rights, essential when building a luxury brand. We now promoted the fact that we had a shop-in-shop at Neiman Marcus, the most prestigious retailer in the world at the time. Only a few highly selected brands were given this honor, and we were one of them. Furthermore, on the floors above that downtown Dallas store sat the entire executive team of Neiman Marcus corporation. They were our primary customer base at the shop. Some of the relationships I developed there became very important to our future.

The most relevant example occurred during one of my visits to Dallas. An older gentleman asked me if we could refurbish an old sterling silver shaving brush his father had given him. Once in a while, we renovated old brushes for customers because of valuable material or for sentimental reasons. I asked the gentleman to leave the brush with me to see what I could do. We sent the brush to Germany and had the finest badger hair put in. On my following trip to Dallas, I caught up with the gentleman and gave him the shaving brush, which was brand new now. He offered to pay, but I insisted it was our pleasure to refurbish his brush at no charge.

A few months later, I was meeting with the men's furnishings buyer in his office. He was the purchasing agent for the merchandise we sold at the Dallas shop. It was an exception to the rule, as all men's grooming falls under the women's cosmetics buyer's responsibility. Since the cosmetic buyer refused to entertain the idea of rolling out TAOS in other Neiman Marcus stores, I asked the men's furnishing buyer to bring the brand under his department. He flatly refused, explaining it was impossible as this would cause a major political rift with the head of the cosmetic buying department. I argued that it made no sense for men's grooming products to be bought by women's cosmetics. Men's buyers should purchase men's grooming brands and put them on the men's floor like every other men's product Neiman Marcus sells. Although the argument made sense, it ultimately challenged the status quo and an industry standard across all department stores. Just before I was about to give up, the older gentleman whose brush I had refurbished came in and introduced himself as the Global VP of men's. He greeted me by my first name. His team was surprised their boss knew me so well. They briefed him on my crazy request. The VP pondered the dilemma and said, "Gentlemen, sometimes we ask for permission, and other times we ask for forgiveness. This is one of those times. Let's do it." I walked out with a $150,000 order to roll out TAOS at sixteen Neiman Marcus locations, half of their total stores back then.

This was a massive win for us. They say no good deed goes unpunished, but in my experience, the opposite can also be true.

In 2000, we secured a small line of credit with Merrill Lynch Bank in Fort Lauderdale. We opened our first free-standing store outside New York City a few months later. The store was located in Miami, Florida, in one of the country's most prestigious malls, Bal Harbour Shops.

This was another significant strategic move to position our company as a luxury brand and start a national retail rollout. The store was off to a good start, prompting me to consider moving our life and business operations back to Miami. New York City was a great place to start a business, but I wanted a different lifestyle. It was also too expensive to operate a distribution center in the city. Commuting to Queens or Brooklyn for work was not an option for me.

We decided to move our headquarters to Miami in August 2001, to scale our retail concept nationally and eventually globally.

We wanted to fly ... but it was premature.

CHAPTER 11

Don't Let a Crisis Go to Waste

"It was the worst day we have ever seen, but it brought out the best in all of us."

—John Kerry

By August 15, 2001, TAOS's new Miami headquarters was up and running. Myriam and I traveled to Los Angeles and Las Vegas a few weeks later to visit potential new store locations. Again, we didn't have the funding to open stores on the other side of the country, but that never stopped us before.

Remember, I was only thirty-three and still operating without deep business experience. Upon completing our West Coast tour, we flew back to NYC on September 10, 2001. The following day, on September 11, 2001, Myriam was having a cup of tea in our NYC apartment when she felt the building shake and the defining roaring noise of an airplane overhead. A few minutes later, on TV, the news broke about a plane that had crashed into one of the twin towers. She looked out our window on the thirty-fifth floor of a high-rise building to see the same image she was watching on the TV screen. Our East 29th Street apartment had an unobstructed view of the towers, which were five miles south of us.

Myriam woke me up and told me what was happening. I jumped out of bed, rushed to our balcony, and stared at the towers in disbelief. It was a picture-perfect morning with a blue sky and clear visibility as far as the eye could see. In the distance, I could see a plane flying away from the towers. Then, the plane made a U-turn back toward the towers. Then, the aircraft went out of sight behind the towers briefly. What happened next shocked the whole world; a ball of fire came out the other side of tower two.

Intuitively, I shouted to Myriam, "Terrorists, terrorists, we are under attack!" We both stood on our balcony speechless, looking at the two towers burning. We could hear sirens from the street down below. I decided to go downstairs to buy a disposable camera. When I returned to my balcony to take the first picture, one of the towers was coming down. We were beyond shocked. My eyes were seeing something that my brain could not comprehend. It was unbelievable even as the scene unfolded in front of us and on television. *There would only be one twin tower remaining.* But to my shock, the second tower crumbled a few minutes later. Chaos was ensuing. When we stepped outside our apartment later on, we saw police cars, fireman trucks heading downtown, and army vehicles in NYC for the first time ever. It reminded me of a scene out of a *Godzilla* movie.

Our attention shifted to our employees' safety, especially those who worked near the tower at our Wall Street store. Earlier that morning, we recommended they lock the store and remain inside. Now we couldn't reach them as all the phone lines in the city were down. We were sick with worry for their well-being. We instructed all other employees to close their stores and go home. That evening, we checked in with all our employees, many of whom had no family in town. Our Wall Street staff had left the store when the towers came down and walked for hours, alongside thousands of other people all covered in dust, to reach their homes.

Fortunately, all our employees were safe. One of our employee's daughters worked in a cafeteria on the 96th floor of the South Tower. Early on September 11, she argued with her manager and quit her job. She was in a subway car when all her coworkers perished. She was the only survivor of floor 96. One of our friends was on the phone with his fiancé, who was on the roof of the North Tower when it collapsed. Everyone who was in NYC that day has stories of 9/11 like these. It was a terrible day.

Since 100 percent of our profit came from Manhattan, how would this affect us? We had moved our headquarters to Miami a few weeks earlier. The next day, we met all our employees at the Madison Avenue store to support each other during those difficult times. While we were there, to our surprise, a customer walked in to buy some shaving cream. We all looked at him, surprised. I felt like saying, "Don't you know what's happening in the city?" Instead, we politely told him that we were closed for business due to the attacks and to please come back another day. That customer had given me some hope the business would be OK.

We needed to get back to Miami, but no one was allowed to enter or leave New York City, and all flights were grounded. A week later, when the situation settled down and the stores opened again, we rented a car to drive to Miami.

Businesses in New York City rebounded faster than we expected. By October, our numbers were almost back on track. We were beyond relieved, but the events of September 11 had left us traumatized. For months, I felt down and lacked motivation for work.

We didn't like our apartment in Miami Beach, which overlooked a parking lot and a supermarket. I felt I needed a lifestyle boost starting with a newer apartment with nice views in a more pleasant neighborhood. After all, that was why I decided to move back to Miami in the first place. We found a beautiful condo in a new luxury building in South Beach. It had a 180-degree view of the ocean, the port of Miami, and the Miami skyline. That building was featured in the opening credits of the *CSI Miami* TV show. The rent was above our budget, but the apartment was the lifestyle I sought. Myriam loved it, but was concerned we wouldn't be able to afford the rent. I thought, "We can't afford *not* to rent this place." Since we met, Myriam and I have lived in various humble apartments in Miami Beach and NYC. But now the business was generating solid profits and the unit was not that much above our budget. In 2002, many foreigners were buying condos in Miami that were left empty. This caused rents to be very low for the quality of the apartments you could get. Living in such a lovely place would boost our morale and motivate us to achieve more with our business. Maybe it was a coincidence, but when we moved into the condo in 2002, our wholesale business started to take off.

Our Wall Street store was not doing well, and the events of 9/11 made it worse. We were on the hook with Deutsche Bank, our landlord, for $800k on our ten-year lease. Retail in the financial district had been impacted negatively, which caused landlords to be more lenient with tenants. We took the opportunity to get out of our lease without penalties, and we walked away, only responsible for the security deposit.

That crisis also made me reconsider our national retail growth strategy. Building stores nationwide would require lots of cash, which

I didn't have, and lots of time on airplanes, which was the last place I wanted to be considering the recent world events. Based on those two factors, I decided to pivot our strategy from national retail expansion to wholesale, which was starting to show traction and required much fewer investments to scale.

The timing could not have been better. The buzz on the street was that men's grooming was the next emerging trend in the beauty industry. A British journalist had coined the word "metrosexual" in an article that went viral in the US media. Men's grooming was a white space; no other men's brand had taken the market leader position and we were perfectly positioned to grab the top spot. And we did.

Almost every retailer we pitched gave us a purchase order. By the end of 2002, TAOS was sold in more than 350 stores, including Nordstrom, Bloomingdales, Saks Fifth Avenue, and many smaller premium specialty shops. We became the men's grooming anchor brand for department stores across the United States.

By the end of 2003, our products were distributed in eight hundred stores nationwide. We reached a huge milestone when TAOS became the number-one selling men's brand at Barneys New York. Brand awareness grew exponentially due to TAOS's visibility in many stores nationwide and in the press.

We could see that retailers were not as focused on the men's grooming category as we hoped. Premium men's grooming represented a small fraction of the cosmetic industry. It was an afterthought that never materialized as a real driver for department stores. When we forecasted wholesale revenues for the next few years, we realized that our growth rate would not be strong enough with that distribution strategy.

On the other hand, our stores generated twenty to thirty times the annual sales of a nearby department store where our products were sold. Additionally, we had to provide the retailer with a 50 percent margin to buy our products and offer expensive in-store support, making that channel unprofitable. Our stores operated with high revenues, high margins, and strong profitability. I decided it was time to pivot our strategy to scale our company-owned retail stores across the United States.

The shocking events of September 11 were a sad day for our nation. We pray that events like this never happen again. But sometimes, when bad things happen in our lives, they can lead us in a new direction toward great opportunities. To take advantage of these events in our lives, we must develop a mindset that focuses on finding the positive more than basking in the negative of the situation.

It's true that even in the face of adversity, individuals and communities can discover opportunities for growth and positive change. Developing a mindset emphasizing resilience and optimism can be crucial in navigating challenging times.

Fostering a positive mindset requires us to acknowledge the difficulties. But it's so much more than that. From there, we can shift our focus to what can be learned and gained from the situation. This approach empowers individuals to turn challenges into opportunities, contributing to personal development and the betterment of society.

Sometimes, problems are just opportunities in disguise.

CHAPTER 12

The 4 Elements of the Perfect Shave

"Innovation is creativity with a job to do."

—John Emmerling

Since the first customer entered our store in 1996, I knew our sales process was complicated.

It went like this. First, we offered customers a shaving cream to buy. Then, we encouraged the customer to buy a shaving brush to achieve a richer lather with the shaving cream. We offered different shaving brush qualities that ranged from $50 to $1,000, so we had to explain their differences. Then, we presented the virtues of using a pre-shave oil before applying shaving cream to add more protection to the skin. And finally, we had the customer smell the different aromas of our aftershave gels and balms based on their skin types. Those were all the necessary tools and products to achieve the perfect shave. To complete the TAOS experience, we also offered our customers elegant, heavy-weight razors that fit the latest Gillette blade system. It was a grueling sales process even for the best salesperson. The issue was even worse in our wholesale stores since we didn't have trained salespeople to guide customers into buying the entire system, resulting in missed opportunities.

We had an excellent product knowledge and sales training system, but controlling our sales associates' message to customers became more complicated as we grew. We needed something to help us have consistency in our messaging across our entire sales organization.

Back when we were developing the TAOS line of products, we were introduced to a copywriter who was a retired advertising executive, straight from the 1950s era of *Mad Men*. He used to run a famous Madison Avenue advertising agency and he was a wiz at copywriting and storytelling. He helped us write the necessary copy for our product packaging and catalog.

One day, he recommended adopting a battle cry for our brand. He explained that a battle cry is a statement that describes exactly what your brand offers in ten words or less. The statement also had to ring true when someone heard it. Ultimately this statement would cause every company salesperson to say the same thing to customers when asked what TAOS was about.

We hired him to facilitate a two-day brainstorming session with our core team. He then provided a complete branding report with fifty battle cry options. One of the battle cries he submitted caught our attention. It embodied precisely what we were about: The 4 Elements of the Perfect Shave. We decided to go with it and added the words that describe the four steps: protect, lather up, shave, and moisturize.

The ad executive explained that now that we had found our battle cry, we had to use it *everywhere*. First, we had to teach this battle cry to every employee in the company. They had to know it by heart. Even if we snuck into their house in the middle of the night and woke them up to ask them what our battle cry is, they should be able to say the slogan without hesitation and with the exact words we had chosen. No variations were allowed. He encouraged us to put this battle cry on our website, our catalogs, and anywhere else it was visible.

At that moment, I realized we needed to start selling our products as a shaving system, not as separate items. We still sold items separately for repeat purchases. This epiphany led us to create a shaving set packaged together, which we named "The Perfect Shave Kit," with our battle cry written prominently on the front of the box. We priced the kits at $100 each, a sweet spot for our customers' average purchases. We also made an introductory Perfect Shave starter kit with smaller-sized products at a retail price of $25 each to encourage trial at a profit. The kits included a pre-shave oil, shaving cream, brush, and aftershave. The two kits in four essential oil aromas became the perfect gift for men during the holiday season.

Our motto in the stores for The Perfect Shave kits was to stack them high and see them fly.

This combination of the battle cry and The Perfect Shave kits triggered our business to grow at warp speed. We felt we had turned our business from a floating barge into a pointy rocket ship. Our sales took off, led by The Perfect Shave kits, which continued to drive and dominate TAOS sales for the rest of the company's life. It also made a majority of customers adopt our whole shaving system and experience The Perfect Shave, instead of parts of it. This, in turn, caused even more loyalty from our customer base.

I knew that innovation and being uniquely differentiated from all other competitors in your industry is the building block of some of the most famous companies in the world. Breakthrough product innovation is at the core of creating an iconic consumer brand.

But this experience taught me an important new lesson.

Until then, I thought innovation was limited to new products we developed. However, The Perfect Shave Kit was not a new product; it was an innovative way to market and sell existing products. This led me to understand that innovation lives in the fiber of our company's culture. Innovation can exist in our products and services, but it can also exist in every aspect of our business.

An example of this was the built-in ring we added to The Perfect Shave single pack samples. The kits gave us the idea to create a beautiful tri-fold that contains single-use samples of pre-shave oil, shaving cream, and aftershave balm. The innovation was that it had a built-in ring at the top of the tri-fold so the sample could be hooked to a clothes hanger. We partnered with Neiman Marcus to hang The Perfect Shave sample on each suit or shirt that was altered for their customers during the thirty days of their in-circle event. This program reached tens of thousands of potential customers. When customers opened their garment bags, they found our samples hanging there for them to try. This promoted product trials with consumers and sent a message to the industry that we were at the forefront of innovation.

Another example was when the TSA started a liquid policy for travelers. Only products with less than 3.4 ounces were allowed to be carried on an airplane. Within two months, we launched our travel shaving products in elegant clear zippered plastic bags with a round sticker that prominently said "TSA Approved." With a minor financial investment, we had just created a new best seller for the company.

With this new outlook on innovation, I began to look for opportunities to innovate in all areas of our company, ensuring that this message was communicated with our employees and ingrained in our company's culture. I reminded everyone on our team, "If it has been done before, we will not do it too. If they go left, we will go right. At least we will be different."

CHAPTER 13

Raising Capital

"The best way to predict the future is to create it."

—Peter Drucker

Beauty brands like L'Occitane were rapidly expanding their retail locations nationally. They operated in smaller retail footprints of five hundred square feet or less, allowing them to secure top locations in the mall's center court while minimizing rent and build-out costs. These small stores generated high sales per square foot because beauty products are not dependent on large store sizes. Some retailers, such as furniture stores, have their revenue directly impacted by the size of the store they operate. On the other hand, beauty retailers sell small items at high prices, making small stores ideal.

Metropolitan cities like New York, Chicago, Boston, Los Angeles, and San Francisco offered great street locations with high foot traffic, but for the rest of the country, malls were the best options for luxury retailers. With that in mind, I started developing a vision for what

TAOS concept could look like in a mall location. After all, our company's first store was only two hundred square feet. A shop that included a barber area requires a larger store size, which was the first thing that had to change. Plus, I thought managing barber service quality nationwide would be difficult. To keep the barber spirit in our mall stores, we could put a barber chair as a window prop or in a corner inside the store to do events when size permitted. On paper, these smaller stores would cost less to operate and build while providing similar sales and profit than larger stores.

Not long after this vision took shape in my head, my real estate agent called to ask if I was interested in a last-minute opportunity to open a shop at the new Columbus Circle vertical mall in New York City's Upper West Side. A retailer had backed out at the last minute and was looking for someone to replace them who could be up and running by the time the mall had its grand opening, which was scheduled a few months later. The mall owner wanted to have more retailers that catered to men and thought the TAOS concept was a great fit. Hugo Boss, Cigar Shop, Tumi, and others were opening stores there. The location inside the mall wasn't ideal, but I thought this would be an excellent opportunity to try our new mall concept. Also, we didn't have stores serving Upper West Side customers in the city yet. The three hundred square foot shop was located on the second floor. The asking rent was within our target budget, so we decided to do it. We managed to open the shop in time for the mall's grand opening in February 2003. The mall, anchored by Whole Foods on the lower level, became very successful. Although our location was out of the main traffic area, we didn't plan for people to have to walk in front of our store on their way to the mall's only bathroom facility. That location, our fourth store, generated more than $3,000 per square foot in its first year with solid profitability without any barber services.

The most important achievement of this store was that it was the first to sell only our branded products. For the first time and after six years in business, we finally manufactured every product sold in our store. From then on, we never sold a third-party brand at TAOS again.

This was the confirmation I needed to roll out the TAOS concept in upscale malls across America.

Our cost to build a store was $250,000 on average. Our cash flow was strong enough to grow organically, but this would limit us to one or two new stores per year. My goal was to exponentially increase our company's revenue by opening one new store every month.

We made our small enterprise a scalable business by sharpening our business model. A scalable business can rapidly ramp up production to meet demand and, at the same time, benefit from economies of scale. Although by 2003, we had a robust wholesale business, Columbus Circle was only our fourth store in operation.

It is not uncommon for businesses to spend years adjusting and refining their business model before achieving scalability. Developing a scalable and profitable business model is a process that involves nonstop learning, adaptation, and sometimes even a complete pivot, as we did more than once during our journey. First, we pivoted from a small store on a side street to a more prominent flagship location on Madison Avenue that added an entire barber shop in the back of the store; then we pivoted away from retail expansion to develop our wholesale division, shifting from being a multibrand retailer to only selling our brand, then finally swinging back to retail with a small footprint shop adapted to malls across America.

People around me felt I was being wishy-washy as a leader. Pivoting frequently like this for a large, established organization can be the kiss of death, but I thought I was making pivots based on new data available to me during our treasure hunt. I felt like a surfer trying to catch the waves. Sometimes, I saw a big wave and rode it. When it fizzled, I found another wave to transport me forward. In hindsight, my flexibility and willingness to pivot were among my strengths as the leader of our organization.

To fine-tune your business model, you may need time to understand your target market, customer needs, and the competitive landscape. This understanding evolves as the business gathers more data and feedback. Our businesses went through several iterations of the business model. Each iteration involved testing hypotheses, learning from failures, and incorporating feedback to make necessary adjustments. Building scalable infrastructure and systems first is critical to achieving scalability. In our case, developing 250 different products under our brand meant it was time to become a branded retailer.

Since opening that many stores required a serious capital infusion, we decided to raise our first round of funding. I had delayed raising capital in the first eight years to avoid high-equity dilution. I wanted to retain as much equity as possible until my exit. For this reason, we decided to raise capital from private investors in our network.

Seed capital, or the first round of funding, is often called a "friends and family round." This means you are going after something other than the professional investor route made up of venture capital or private equity funds. Even though it is called a friends and family round, it doesn't mean you have to raise money from friends and family, although many people do. It involves raising funds from private individuals that are part of your network. These can be high-net-worth individuals you already know or are introduced to. This round typically occurs in the early stages of a business when traditional funding sources like banks or venture capitalists may not yet be accessible or, in some cases, desirable.

A private friends and family round is often less formal than later fundraising stages. Entrepreneurs may seek support from those close to them to cover initial start-up costs, product development, market research, and other essential expenses during the early stages of the business. In our case, it was to fund the first round of national store expansion.

The investment is often based on trust and belief in the entrepreneur rather than a detailed business plan. Private investors know the risks involved in supporting a start-up or new business, and their investment is often seen as a vote of confidence in the entrepreneur's vision. However, they also stand to gain if the business succeeds. Due diligence in a friends and family round may be less extensive than in later funding rounds. The funding may be structured as either convertible notes or equity. In a convertible note, the investment is considered a loan that can convert into equity at a later funding round.

Successful seed capital fundraising can provide the initial traction needed to attract other investors. Entrepreneurs need to approach friends and family rounds with transparency and clear communication. While this type of funding can be a valuable source of initial capital, managing expectations and clearly outlining the risks involved are crucial. Additionally, legal documentation, even if less formal than in later rounds, is advisable to avoid potential misunderstandings and disputes in the future.

Bringing in investors for the first time meant things were going to be different from now on. For one thing, we would no longer be the sole shareholder of TAOS. This meant we had to draw up a purchase agreement contract and an operating agreement contract, among others, to finalize the deal. Fortunately, I had an experienced legal counsel to help me navigate these uncharted territories. I instinctively knew two things: one was that I would never concede control of my company to anyone until I sold the business, and two I would never sign contracts that required giving personal guarantees. With that in mind, we drafted documents to protect such things from ever happening.

Today, as a business coach, I often encounter entrepreneurs in hairy situations. The majority of the time, they are in dire straits because they signed a contract with an investor, or multiple investors, that contained clauses putting them in unwanted positions later on. This usually happens because investors have an upper hand. They have more experience with the process than the entrepreneur and they draft contracts that protect *them* more than their counterpart.

One such example is a young man who raised $350,000 from a private lender with whom he signed a document that would enable the lender to take 100 percent of the business equity if his loan was in default.

Another example is an entrepreneur whose board fired her after she built the company from zero to $25 million during the past eighteen years.

This is a major pitfall for entrepreneurs raising money because they usually need the money before a certain deadline. Since the process of raising money usually takes longer than expected, it puts the entrepreneur in a more desperate financial position. Without money, entrepreneurs tend to not hire top lawyers to draft or negotiate contracts, leaving the investor to have a one-sided contract in their favor. To mitigate this, be critical of any contract you sign, have a good lawyer on your side, and give yourself time to go through the fundraising process, as it almost always takes more time than expected.

Our CFO and CPA firm introduced me to five successful local real estate developers. They asked me to pitch the investors personally because they knew I had the passion and ability to sell our company's vision. I pitched five local high-net-worth individuals who had made their fortune in real estate. Four of them agreed to invest. Within thirty days, we closed on a $2.5 million round at a $40 million valuation. The process took less than two months, which I later realized was extremely fast and not the norm for most entrepreneurs. At the time, it showed that TAOS was being perceived as a strong brand with excellent growth prospects.

With a full war chest, we kicked off our retail expansion. We started with the Las Vegas real estate convention, where Myriam and I performed our dog and pony show in front of the country's largest shopping mall owners, including Simon Properties, General Growth, Macerich, Taubman, and others. Our pitch was simple but effective. "If you want to attract more men to your mall, you need to give men more reasons to visit your mall. Nobody needs another women's clothing or shoe store. What you need is something different, something you don't find in every mall, and something like, you guessed it, The Art of Shaving." Again, the timing was perfect.

The same spirit to go after the emerging male consumers we experienced with wholesale was also present in the minds of the mall owners. Some agreed to offer us locations immediately and others promised they would let us know about upcoming available leases as soon as they found out. It didn't take long to start executing leases from coast to coast. In 2005, we opened multiple stores, and by 2006, we were opening ten to twelve per year in some of the world's most prestigious and expensive retail real estate.

Most of our stores generated solid and profitable sales, igniting even more sales growth in our company.

This rocket ship was ready for takeoff.

Columbus Circle store, 2003

CHAPTER 14

Extraordinary People

"Surround yourself with the best people you can find, delegate authority, and don't interfere as long as the policy you've decided upon is being carried out."

—Ronald Reagan

Hiring people was not one of my strengths. I made many mistakes in that area, but over the years, we were still able to assemble a great cast of passionate characters who were instrumental in building our company.

Attracting, retaining, and managing talent is one of the most complex parts of building a business. The reason, in my opinion, is that it is the only element of the business that depends on human beings, and human beings are not easy to manage. Growing exponentially with employees in remote locations nationwide made this even more challenging. We had three to five employees per store on average, with one or two stores per city. Every day we had to ensure that each store was opened on time, staffed adequately, and efficiently produced sales.

In addition to all our stores, we ran a vertical operation in our Miami headquarters that included a laboratory, a distribution center, a finance and administration department, a supply chain, R&D, marketing, a wholesale division, and retail management teams.

A mentor who was a famous headhunter for Fortune 500 companies once explained to me that if salespeople did their job, I wouldn't need a store manager. If the manager did their job, we would not need a regional manager, and if that person did their job well, we wouldn't need a VP of retail. He put in plain words that Myriam and I, as owners, could run our two stores better than anyone we could hire, but that would limit us to two stores running at 100 percent. If we wanted to grow big, we had to get used to the idea that our employees would run our stores at 80 percent, but 80 percent of a hundred stores is much more than 100 percent of two stores.

I understood his words of wisdom. I needed to create an organization to support running and scaling our business.

Many entrepreneurs are challenged by the transition from mom-and-pop to small businesses to medium-sized enterprises. This transition requires the organization to create processes, structure, and accountability in order to scale and run the business successfully. Without achieving this transformation, a business cannot grow or, on the other hand, it could have growing pains.

In 1997, we hired our first employee. Ten years later, we had more than 250 employees. Three years after that, when we left TAOS, our headcount reached more than four hundred employees.

In 2005, while trying to grow our company exponentially, I only had two people on my management team. A retail national sales manager and a wholesale director. Myriam and I handled everything else. Our retail manager was a great guy we recruited from MAC cosmetics to run our stores. To my disappointment, he quit after one year to pursue his academic studies. I replaced him with a seasoned retailer who came from apparel retail. I soon realized she was not a good fit for our organization and wasn't liked by our retail staff, which could end up being a disaster in that world. I let her go and took over running our stores myself, on top of all my other responsibilities.

Our wholesale director, who had recently joined the company, was an industry veteran with an abrasive personality, but I was stretched so thin that I kept her longer than I should have.

I was running and growing a $10 million business solo without a management team to support me. I was managing production, inventory planning, distribution, finance, and store operations. I was overwhelmed with the workload and I was not in a good position to grow our company exponentially.

Around that time, someone recommended I read the book *Good to Great* by Jim Collins. That book was timely and among the most impactful business books I had ever read up to that point in my career. It somehow unlocked something in my head relating to people and culture that had held us back for a long time.

The book discussed "having the right people on the bus and in the right seat." This metaphor emphasizes the importance of assembling a talented and effective team to achieve organizational success.

The critical element of Jim Collins's concept includes ensuring that your team members possess the necessary skills and talents relevant to their roles. This involves recruiting individuals with the right expertise and capabilities while considering the alignment of individuals with the organization's values and culture. Team members who share common values are more likely to collaborate effectively. Team members should be committed to the overall purpose and goals of the organization. Their dedication contributes to a shared vision and each team member should be assigned a role leveraging their strengths and expertise. Placing people in positions that align with their skills enhances overall team performance. Finally, consider the compatibility between an individual's skills, personality, and the requirements of the specific role to ensure that team members are best suited to their responsibilities.

By combining these elements, organizations can create a cohesive and high-performing team. The metaphor suggests that a company's success is not just about having talented individuals but also about ensuring they are in roles that make the best use of their abilities and contribute to the organization's overall success. It emphasizes the strategic placement of individuals to maximize their impact on achieving the organization's objectives.

After reading the book, I was so blown away that I stood up from my desk, walked over to my wholesale director's office, and fired her on the spot.

I had uncovered a huge blind spot, and a sense of clarity came over me. The book showed me the last piece of the puzzle I needed if I wanted to start flying: having the right people in the right seats.

Until then, I had struggled to get by with an army of great soldiers and lieutenants, but to take the company to these new levels, we needed best-in-class generals. I needed to fill five vice president positions: sales, marketing, operations, real estate, and finance.

With our retail strategy proving we had a scalable and profitable business model, I set our company's sail toward a five-year revenue target of $50 million a year.

In order to reach that target, I needed to surround myself with a team of extraordinary people.

I hired one of the top beauty industry headhunters in NYC. Yes, he was expensive and had to be paid with a retainer whether or not I hired anyone. Fortunately, he quickly identified a few candidates for the operations position. Operations and supply chain were areas that required a lot of my time. The résumé of a man, named Kurtis, who ran operations for a well-known beauty brand in Boston stood out among others. He wasn't happy after a conglomerate acquired the brand because he preferred working for a more entrepreneurial company. When I liked a candidate at the end of each interview, I would say, "The only issue with joining our company is that you will have to live in paradise." I hit it off with the Boston guy and I made him an offer that he accepted, and he quickly relocated to Miami to start his new position with the company. Before he joined us and since 1996, I was responsible for operations, which included warehousing, fulfillment, and product manufacturing. I was excited to let go of this responsibility. He turned out to be an incredibly gifted operations manager. He hit the ground running, and for the next three years, I didn't have to worry about operations anymore, putting more of my focus on driving sales. After we were acquired, he was promoted high up within P&G's headquarters in Cincinnati, Ohio.

Our headhunter then introduced me to a gentleman, named Boris, who was the general manager of Neiman Marcus in Bal Harbour, Florida. Boris was a charmingly quirky character with a great sense of humor. He was impeccably dressed from head to toe in the finest Italian men's brands sold at Neiman Marcus. I wanted to hire him as soon as I heard "Neiman Marcus," but I was also very impressed with his devotion to customer experience. This was something he and I had a lot of passion for. Fifteen minutes after he left our office, I called him to say I wanted him to join our company. I sent him an offer the next day, and he immediately accepted it. He later told me he had a great opportunity with Saks Fifth Avenue Mexico City that he had been considering. But because Saks was dragging their feet, and I called him immediately to make him an offer, he decided to join us. He became the face of TAOS for our entire retail division. He was one of the best retailers I had ever met. He taught me much about what he had learned while working for Neiman Marcus for twenty years. He had started as a stock boy and went up the ranks to manage a $100 million business. He was one of our most passionate employees, and we became very close friends. Aside from our successful collaboration, working with him was a lot of fun for me and everyone in the company. He had an endearing way of calling me "jefe," which means *boss* in Spanish. He called me that for years, even after I sold the company and was no longer his boss. Sadly, he passed away a few years ago at the young age of fifty-one. I miss him greatly.

One of my employees introduced me to a friend, named Jorge, who had built hundreds of stores for a large public company. He joined TAOS to spearhead all real estate and build-outs for the company. He would go on to build the next hundred-plus TAOS stores.

My operations manager helped me recruit the CFO from his old company. Her name was Stella and she, too, didn't enjoy the culture after their company was acquired. She moved to Miami to run our finance and administration department.

The most challenging position for me to fill was marketing. I eventually hired Gita, but it was just before being acquired, so we didn't have enough time to do great things together.

Throughout the company, from coast to coast, we had an incredible cast of characters that represented TAOS in a passionate and dedicated manner.

They were our brand ambassadors.

My management philosophy was that our people on the front lines were the company's most important employees because they were in direct contact with the customers. Having worked on the front lines myself, I knew how critical our retail sales teams were to the success of the company. Therefore, our management team's job was structured to serve our ambassadors on the front line because they created our success every minute of every day. I would remind our people every chance I had, "We build this company one customer at a time." Without realizing it at the time, we had adopted what is now commonly known as an inverted pyramid.

The concept of the inverted pyramid management style is a model that places frontline employees at the top of the organizational structure. These individuals, often the first point of contact with customers, are empowered with decision-making autonomy, acknowledging their vital role in customer satisfaction and business success. At the base of this pyramid, the top management assumes a role of support and empowerment. They are not commanding overlords but facilitators who provide resources, guidance, and encouragement. This structure cultivates a customer-centric ethos, ensuring that every strategy and decision aligns with the ultimate goal of fulfilling customer needs. Moreover, it champions open communication and collaborative spirit, creating an environment where feedback is not just encouraged but a cornerstone of continuous improvement. The inverted pyramid is a philosophy that places trust and responsibility in the hands of those who are most intimately connected with the market—a game-changing perspective for entrepreneurs aiming to build customer-focused organizational cultures.

It was a beautiful thing to experience our company culture and to see how it impacted our success. I remember interviewing applicants who would say they wanted to work for our company because they knew one of our employees who was so happy working here. That was music to my ears, as I had aimed to create the type of company that employees didn't dread working for.

I still hear from many of our past employees, from time to time, who recall fond memories of their time with TAOS. The greatest compliment to me is when past employees reach out to see if there are opportunities to work with Myriam and me again.

Even after we grew to a few hundred employees, I insisted on speaking to every candidate at least for a minute or two before the employment was confirmed with our company. I wanted to be a gatekeeper in case I had a horrible feeling when I spoke to someone, which rarely happened. I thought if I enjoyed spending a few minutes with this person, our customers would enjoy it too. But also, I wanted to send a strong message that I cared about who represented the brand and that everyone in our company is essential to our success.

Cultivating a great company culture is one of the foundational pillars of success. This begins with clearly articulating your core values and mission, leaning on one compass to guide every action and decision. Our values and mission were based on promoting healthy natural living, being customer-focused, being innovative in everything we do, and creating a workplace that made people excited to come to work.

Someone I respect said to me, "Culture equals cash." Culture was always critical to me, and I worked on it daily. Culture is not a project you work on; it is something you live and breathe every day. Once you tap into that magic, it can profoundly impact your business success.

I was excited that I was able to put a strong management team together so quickly. With my team in place, I went into my office, closed the door, and realized I had nothing to do now that I had delegated all my day-to-day responsibilities. I had someone taking care of the stores better than I ever did, someone to handle all supply chain and operations better than I ever did. Someone was managing finance and administration better than I ever did and there were now people who were responsible for store build-outs and marketing better than I ever did.

I stayed in my office for two days until I realized that now that I had a team to run the day-to-day business, I had just become the CEO of TAOS. Yes, I had the title for many years but I was never in a position to be a CEO.

Like many entrepreneurial founders, I gave myself the CEO job from day one. I didn't have to interview against a pool of qualified candidates for the position, which sometimes implies we may not be the ideal person for the job. In other cases, a founder's skills may have been perfect to get the company to a particular stage, but other skills may be necessary to get the company to the next level. This is not an easy realization for a controlling business founder to make.

I asked myself, what does a CEO do exactly?

I concluded that the CEO's responsibilities were to create a vision for the company, ensure that he has the resources to achieve that vision, recruit everyone internally and externally with his vision, and lead his people to achieve the vision. Since 1996, I have always worked as a member of the business's day-to-day operations. Now, I was in a position to work exclusively on scaling the business. And that is precisely what I started doing.

From 2006 to 2008, we tripled our company's sales from $10 million to $30 million.

We were flying!

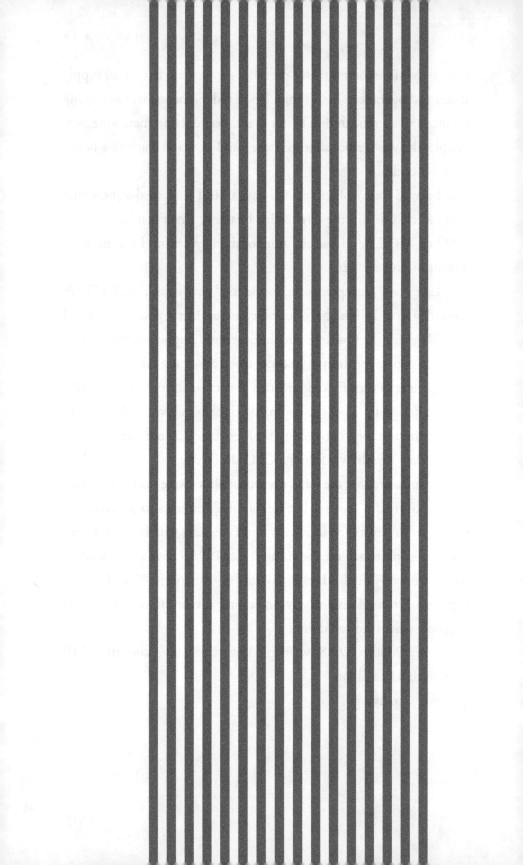

CHAPTER 15

Rocket Fuel

"Sometimes you have to play with the big boys to realize you are one."

—Unknown

In 2005, our friends and family round funded the opening of twelve new TAOS stores across the United States, including Los Angeles, Las Vegas, Atlanta, Miami, and Dallas. The majority of our new stores were performing very well with a direct profit contribution per store of more than 30 percent each.

We had created a proven specialty retail concept with a potential for two hundred stores nationwide.

To keep the momentum of rolling out new stores each month, we needed to raise growth capital (rocket fuel) to fund the next phase of our expansion.

We had reached a stage perfectly positioned to raise a Series A round with professional investors.

To run the process, we hired a midsize investment bank out of Chicago with industry experience led by a young, dynamic person I instantly liked. I aimed to raise $15 million at an $80 million valuation. Five million dollars would go to us personally to take chips off the table, and the remaining $10 million would be used to fund business growth. One of the things I always recommend doing is keeping some of the raised funds for yourself. Professional investors are very open to this as they like their CEO/founders to feel less pressure by reducing their risk, which in turn allows the CEO to perform better on the job.

The investment bankers prepared a good pitch deck and started making introductions to a select group of venture funds specializing in beauty. Three of them submitted offers right away, competing for our deal. Given my lack of experience in investment terms, I relied heavily on my banker and my trusted lawyer for guidance.

Ultimately, I selected a Boston private equity firm for two reasons that felt important to me then. The first reason was because they promised not to interfere with how we were running our business. Arrogant as it sounds, I felt confident in my ability to lead the company to the finish line. The second reason was that they structured their investment as a convertible mezzanine loan that would allow me to retain more equity.

I might have chosen a different offer with more equity dilution if I had more experience in mergers and acquisitions (M&A). The mezzanine terms allowed us to personally have a better outcome if we sold the business at a higher price, while we would do worse at a lower exit amount since their investment was structured with high interest rates that could convert to preferred equity in the company. Because of the high interest, we asked to draw the $10 million investment in three tranches to avoid incurring interest until we needed the money. This turned out to be another big mistake.

When entrepreneurs raise venture capital funds, many are untrained in the complicated area of M&A. This puts entrepreneurs in a precarious position, which can be compounded when they are in dire need of cash to continue funding the business.

Entrepreneurs often have the misperception that the investment bankers on their team are looking out for their best interest. I am not saying bankers are not looking out for you. They have good intentions and want the best for all parties involved, but their interest and their clients' interests are not entirely aligned. While they tend to do many deals with investors in their network, they will typically only do one deal with you, and regardless of the agreement terms you sign, they usually get paid a success fee. Also, their commission doesn't increase much whether you raise $15 million or $17 million, and when it comes to valuation, their commission is the same at any level.

My investment bankers ran a great process, but in hindsight, I wish I had someone experienced looking out for my best interest with no commission on the transaction.

To start the flying stage of a small business, raising Series A funding stands as a landmark achievement, often symbolizing a transition from a start-up to a more established entity. However, this road is fraught with complexities that demand careful navigation. One of the foremost challenges you'll encounter is the dilution of ownership. As investors infuse capital into your business, your stake diminishes, potentially altering the balance of control and influence. This transition is not merely financial but also psychological, as the influx of external funds brings with it heightened expectations and pressures to perform.

Moreover, the fundraising process itself is a double-edged sword. While it offers the much-needed fuel for growth, it is inherently complex and time-consuming. It diverts your focus from day-to-day business operations, embroiling you in negotiations, legalities, and the art of pitching. This phase also tests your vision's alignment with your investors. It's essential to ensure that your investors not only bring in the capital but also share your values and long-term objectives, lest you find yourself in a tug-of-war over the company's direction.

Another subtlety lies in the art of valuation. Overvaluation, while tempting, can backfire in future funding rounds, particularly if your business doesn't scale at the anticipated pace. This could lead to unfavorable conditions in subsequent funding endeavors, commonly known as a "down round." Furthermore, stepping into the arena of Series A funding subjects your business to increased scrutiny and demands for transparency, elevating the level of reporting and administrative rigor.

As an entrepreneur, it's essential to weigh these considerations meticulously. Balancing the need for capital against maintaining control and adherence to your core vision is a delicate act. It often benefits from the wisdom of mentors, the insights of fellow entrepreneurs, and the guidance of legal and financial experts. Raising Series A funding is not just about securing capital; it's about charting a course that keeps your entrepreneurial spirit and vision at the helm, steering your venture toward sustainable growth and success.

To my unpleasant surprise, I quickly found out that the investors we had were the exact type that gave venture capitalists a lousy reputation. They were predatory in their approach, to say the least, prying on small, hardworking entrepreneurs. To best take advantage of us, their closing documents, including the operating agreement, were filled with ambushes disguised as restrictive covenants. Those clauses were intended to put us in a vulnerable position; when we defaulted each time, we tripped one of them. In fact, we tripped one of their clauses the day after closing on our transaction. They immediately tried to take advantage of our default, but I pushed back. From that day on, we became adversaries instead of partners. I didn't like their unethical approach to doing business, which greatly contradicted my philosophy. I believe in win-win relationships in business and my personal life.

Having said that, I am grateful for their investment in our company, which enabled us to turbocharge the business toward our final exit.

Unfortunately, the investors I chose were wolves in sheep's clothing. Unfortunately for them, I fight like a tiger.

CHAPTER 16

Fifty-Seven Billion Dollars

"The best a man can get."

—Gillette tagline

In 2005, while I was busy growing TAOS, P&G acquired Gillette and its portfolio of brands, including Old Spice, Braun, and Venus, for $57 billion. To this day, it was and still is the largest acquisition of any consumer-packaged brand in history.

It is hard to believe that, during its prosperous 180-year history, P&G sold products exclusively for women. Overnight, the Gillette acquisition made P&G the world's leading men's grooming company, with a 28 percent market share of the global men's grooming market. They had become the largest consumer goods company in the world without ever marketing products to half the world's population: men. For this reason, P&G's leadership declared "Winning with Men" as their top strategic priority for the future.

At the time of the acquisition, Gillette accounted for 70 percent of the market share of blades sold worldwide. Since then, it has dropped to 55 percent due to increased competition and men's beard trends.

At the same time, TAOS was a thriving shaving brand leader in the premium segment of the US market.

This placed TAOS and Gillette brands on a direct strategic collision course.

Gillette's first launch under P&G was the highly anticipated new technology: the Fusion blades system. The Fusion5 blade was Gillette's latest five-blade cartridge razor blade. Since we fitted our hand-crafted razor with the latest Gillette blades, I tasked my PR director to get their hands on a sample of the new blade as soon as possible. We wanted a Fusion system on our expensive razor before our competitors.

Our team contacted Gillette's PR agency, assuming they would have PR samples available pre-launch. They refused due to the level of secrecy surrounding the new blade. Given the skepticism about the need for Fusion to have five blades on a razor, they asked if I could provide my expert opinion, which they thought would go a long way to change the media narrative.

We agreed, and Gillette's PR representatives secretly met me at a NYC hotel, where I was asked to empty my pockets and hand over my cell phone. It felt more like a CIA operation than a razor test. I was excited to be one of a handful of people to try the Fusion razor before it was released to the general public. I have to admit, after trying it, I was very impressed with the new five-blade razor.

In the end, we couldn't get our hands on a blade sample before launch, but we did secure a PR opportunity for me to appear on CNN to provide my impression of Fusion.

The next day, I was on air on CNN, where I was asked for my opinion on the new Fusion blade, which would launch in US retailers a few days later. P&G's Men's Grooming president happened to be watching CNN that day. With billions of dollars on the line, he asked his team, "Who is this guy talking about our product on CNN?" They explained I was the CEO of a luxury shaving brand.

A few weeks later, P&G sent two executives to meet with me in Miami. Over a cup of coffee, they complimented me on TAOS brand and its successes and asked me if we would be interested in a collaboration between our companies. It was great to hear this because our company had been promoting Gillette blade systems exclusively on our high-end razor for the past ten years. I said, "Yes, we would love to." They asked if I had any idea what that would look like. Without much hesitation, I said, "Yes, we should launch a co-branded premium razor together."

After that meeting, I felt as if I was being recruited to the big leagues.

I was on top of the world.

Back in Boston, they received the green light to pursue the collaboration. They quickly started negotiating and drafting a complex eighty-page licensing agreement. A few months later, we signed a licensing deal with P&G to become the first company in the history of Gillette to be awarded a license of their brand name. We were given the worldwide exclusivity of the Gillette brand for the premium marketplace. This included everything outside of mass-market retail. It was an extraordinary honor and another massive milestone for our little company.

We collaborated with Gillette's incredible design team, and they grilled Myriam and me, knowing we had in-depth insight into the premium male consumer. Like in the early days of creating our first shaving products, we knew exactly what our customers wanted in a razor. We knew because our customers had told us a thousand times.

During a four-hour meeting, Myriam and I described the perfect razor to the design team. We covered every detail, from weight and balance to colors and finishes. True to themselves, P&G needed complex data to support our recommendations. They hired a marketing consulting firm to run an entire panel focus group with a price tag that was hundreds of thousands of dollars. Two months later, the consultants provided consumer feedback to P&G. The report confirmed all our recommendations. We thought it was a waste of money, but we appreciated the disciplined approach P&G is famous for.

Myriam and I came up with the Fusion Chrome Collection (FCC) name and Gillette approved it. The collection utilized some of Gillette's technologies that were not yet available to the public, such as a vibrating handle and a light technology that allowed the user to see where he was shaving. The product would be co-branded: Gillette and The Art of Shaving.

Our contract had a sales target of fifty thousand units for year one at a blended price point of $150 in retail and $75 in wholesale. Gillette traditionally struggled to sell razor handles above $12, so this was an exciting test for them. They were also used to selling millions of units. During production meetings, they often accidentally said fifty million units instead of fifty thousand, which made everyone laugh.

FCC launched in early 2007. We did a PR event in a suite at a chic NYC hotel to promote the new product and high-visibility strategic alliance. We invited eighty-five writers and editors of major media outlets for the unveiling of FCC and to meet and greet Myriam, me, and top Gillette representatives. Eighty-three editors showed up. Gillette PR executives were blown away as they had never experienced such a press turnout. We received tremendous media mentions for this collaboration, and the products were hugely successful with consumers and retailers.

By the end of the first year, FCC accounted for almost 20 percent of our total revenue. I started feeling dependent on the Gillette relationship, which made me uncomfortable. I was well aware of the risk when I agreed to the collaboration. The risk was that if FCC were successful, Gillette would try to acquire us, but we would lose some negotiating leverage due to our dependence on P&G. That was a risk I had to take, and I did it without hesitation. The opportunity was too great to pass up.

In 2007 and 2008, TAOS was growing exponentially, with sales rising at a rate of 40 percent year over year. We were on a rocket ship well on our way toward hitting $50 million in the next few years. It was exhilarating.

In January 2008, I met with P&G's president of Male Grooming in Boston for a one-on-one meeting. During our meeting, the president leaned over and asked me, "Eric, would you be interested in selling us TAOS?"

I made a conscious effort to maintain my composure because, at that moment, all my life's hard work, successes, failures, fears, and anxiety that came with achieving my dreams of one day being in this very position was about to come true against all odds.

It was a moment I will never forget.

I responded calmly, "I appreciate the offer, but before giving you an answer, I first need to discuss it with my partner and investors."

I left his office and immediately called Myriam to tell her what had happened.

We were both in disbelief…and beyond excited!

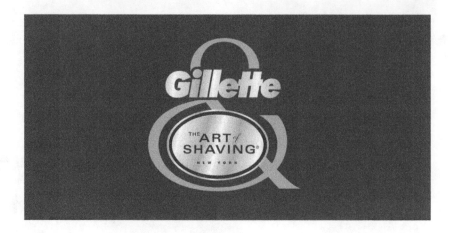

The Gillette and The Art of Shaving collaboration logo

The Fusion Chrome Collection

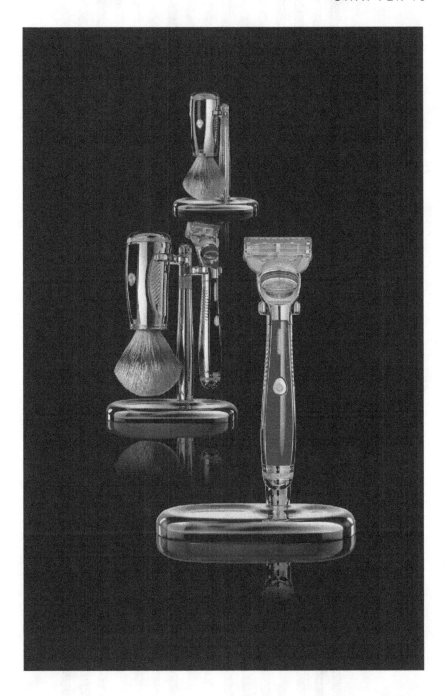

CHAPTER 17

Untrained to Slay the Dragon

"Fairy tales do not tell children that dragons exist. Children already know that dragons exist. Fairy tales tell children dragons can be killed."

—G. K. Chesterton

Like all good fairy-tale stories, adversity lurks just around the corner.

I had spent the previous twenty-three years obsessed with building and positioning a company that could one day be sold, but I never really thought about preparing myself for M&A. It's like achieving your dream of playing in the Super Bowl, except you were never trained to play football. I was untrained to slay the dragon and face the most incredible opportunity of my career.

It's common for entrepreneurs to find themselves inexperienced in M&A when selling their business. Running a business and navigating the complexities of M&A transactions are very different skills, and at the time of M&A, entrepreneurs may have yet to gain prior experience in the intricacies of selling a company.

Entrepreneurs typically focus on building and running their businesses and becoming experts in their industry, and they are understandably focused on the day-to-day operations, customer satisfaction, and financial management. When it comes to legal matters, negotiations, and the complexities of M&A transactions, they may need more specialized knowledge, and this is exactly where I was.

It doesn't help matters that most entrepreneurs have a deep personal and emotional connection to their business, which can cloud objective decision-making during the sale process. To compensate for this, entrepreneurs can engage professionals specializing in M&A, such as investment bankers, attorneys, and accountants, who are deeply experienced in these processes. Sometimes it can even be helpful to recruit the guidance of an entrepreneur who has exited their business and has gone through this process before.

The M&A process can be very distracting to entrepreneurs and CEOs. I was advised to run our business as if we would never sell it because a well-performing business is likely to attract more favorable offers while a poor-performing business can put a seller in a vulnerable position. But the time I was putting in to manage the sale of our business was hindering my ability to stay focused on running our day-to-day business.

Another factor is clearly defining your goals and priorities for the sale. Whether it's maximizing value, ensuring a smooth transition for employees, or other considerations, understanding your objectives will guide the negotiation process. Ensure you are very clear on the bottom price you would accept to sell your company. This means you will reject any bids until the buyer makes an offer at or above your bottom price. Let's say you won't sell your business unless you receive a $100 million offer. Will you really say no to a $95 million offer? Or even a $90 million offer? This is much harder to do than it sounds.

Another lesson I learned along the way is to understand who has leverage. While leverage can come in many forms, it often falls in the hands of the person who is more motivated to do the deal and who has more time to finalize the transaction.

With this opportunity in front of me, my first thought was to turn to my investors for guidance. Yes, the wolves in sheep's clothing. I figured since they are trained in M&A, this was an area where they could add value.

Without hesitation, my investors recommended that I hire Goldman Sachs to represent us in this transaction. It made sense since, six months earlier, P&G had acquired a large haircare brand with Goldman representing the seller. At first, I didn't like the idea of hiring Goldman because I felt we were too small for them, even with the size of our transaction. In general, I avoid putting myself in a situation where I am a small fish in a big pond. In my previous experience raising funds, I hired a medium-sized investment bank and was working directly with one of the principals of the firm, whereas in a large firm you can end up being represented by a junior executive.

Nevertheless, I stayed open-minded about exploring the idea. I met with the head of Goldman's M&A in New York, who pitched me on their services. I guess they knew from experience what a guy in my position wanted to hear. Based on their last transaction, they valued our company at $180 million. I liked that number a lot and it was based on actual and recent comparative transactions in our industry with strategic buyers.

In March 2008, we decided to hire Goldman to run our process, but I would soon find out that may not have been our best decision.

The first red flag came from our engagement with Goldman when they introduced me to the team handling our transaction. The lead guy was a junior banker with a less-than-appealing personality. I voiced my concerns but was assured that their top executive would stay involved with the transaction at every step. They planned to run a process by bringing other strategic acquirers to see if they could get a bidding war going. I didn't think that was a good idea, but what did I know about M&A?

Goldman took time to prepare the pitch deck and the data room. When it was finally ready, they set up meetings with P&G's M&A team, where I pitched our story and answered questions about TAOS. I did the same with other potential acquirers, including L'Oréal, Estée Lauder, and Energizer, who owns the Edge shaving brand.

At the end of the roadshow, they all politely passed on the opportunity except P&G, who was the only buyer left in the process. We were back where we started a few months earlier. I felt Goldman had wasted valuable time on this transaction.

In July 2008, after giving them access to our data room, P&G submitted a formal offer to acquire TAOS for $80 million in cash. My first reaction was disappointment in the size of the offer. My confirmation bias made me want to believe Goldman's original estimated value of our company was worth $180 million. After discussing the offer with my Goldman team, they returned to P&G to negotiate a higher price. To my surprise, they informed P&G that we had other offers, that their offer was too low, and that they were being removed from the process unless they gave us a higher offer.

P&G's president called me upset and offended by Goldman's insulting negotiation technique. He said they were pulling their offer because he thought we were too far apart on valuation. It was not only insulting, but it was also a terrible strategy. I was surprised a reputable investment bank like Goldman would pull such an amateur move.

Goldman had managed to screw up a deal that we had handed to them on a silver platter. We brought them a great brand with strong growth and a motivated, strategic buyer. All they had to do was negotiate the best terms and get the deal to a close. No games, no drama.

After a few weeks without news, I contacted P&G's president to apologize for Goldman's unacceptable faux pas. He accepted our apology and asked that we formally invite them into our data room to resume the process and start due diligence. We agreed.

P&G's due diligence team started working on our transaction internally in early September 2008. A week later, on September 15, 2008, Lehman Brothers declared bankruptcy, which didn't register since I was not in touch with the financial markets then. P&G had its due diligence team in our Miami offices in late September, when the stock market collapsed due to the subprime mortgage crisis. The Dow Jones industrial average fell 777 points in one day. The world went into a tailspin during what was deemed as the worst financial crisis since the great depression. P&G stock tumbled along with most other publicly traded companies.

The world was upside down.

Most, if not all, M&A deals, including ours, were put on hold. P&G executives pulled their offer for the second time. I blamed Goldman for having dragged the process too long.

To make matters worse, heading into Q4, our business's most important selling season, our sales tumbled 25 percent overnight, as sales did for most other premium retailers. That was an abrupt shift from the extreme growth trend we had experienced during the prior two years. Our problems were compounded by the fact that we were making heavy investments in our expansion.

By the end of December 2008, we had a $3.5 million gap in Q4 sales and in cash flow.

TAOS was running out of cash rapidly, P&G's offer to acquire us was off the table, Bank of America (BoA) threatened to foreclose on our $3 million line of credit, and Myriam was six months pregnant.

Unexpectedly, I was in the worst position I had ever faced in my entrepreneurial career.

CHAPTER 18

Crisis Management

"The secret of crisis management is not good vs. bad; it's preventing the bad from getting worse."

—Andy Gilman

Entrepreneurs are optimistic creatures! This mindset is beneficial to start and grow a business. However, that very mindset can work against entrepreneurs and prevent them from being effective crisis managers. In my experience, entrepreneurs in business trouble usually do too little too late to address or avoid a crisis. Various reasons, including overconfidence, denial, lack of awareness, lack of planning, and resistance to change, can cause this.

Running a growing company requires very different skill sets and mindset than leading a company in crisis mode. I have been through three crises that affected the economy—September 11, the financial crisis, and the pandemic. I was blindsided by the first two. With the third one, no one could predict a pandemic, but I did warn people around me that the next crisis is to be expected. It is more about *when* it is coming than *if* it is coming. We don't know when. We don't know how. But we know they are coming. Getting comfortable with this can help us keep a vigilant posture in our business to avoid getting caught off guard. This can mean many things, including having a cash reserve, staying up to speed with macroeconomic conditions, contingency planning, and seeking professional advice.

While I was obsessively growing our top line to achieve the highest exit possible, we were operating at a loss. Top line (sales) versus bottom line (profits). Where should the focus be? A common dilemma for many entrepreneurs is whether to focus their business strategy on top-line or bottom-line growth. Top-line growth is essential for newer businesses, but this can strain resources. Conversely, focusing too much on bottom-line growth may hinder innovation and market capture. Entrepreneurs must strike a balance between the two, cultivating steady revenue growth while maintaining profitability to ensure long-term success.

A third option, which, in my opinion, is vital, is the "Cash Is King" mindset. This option emphasizes the importance of cash flow in business regardless of whether your focus is on top-line or bottom-line growth. Large companies with CFOs know this well, but entrepreneurs with less sophisticated financial skills often ignore cash management. Running out of cash can cause entrepreneurs to experience high anxiety, a loss of focus, and the over-dilution of equity early in their journey. Maintaining a robust cash position by having a cash reserve should be the top priority for your business. This will ensure its ability to navigate fluctuations in sales revenue, invest in growth, and remain solvent in both good and bad times.

By the way, thinking that increasing sales will solve your cash issue often only worsens matters. That's because your optimistic mind wants to believe what you wish for will come true.

Fortunately for us, we reacted quickly and decisively to this crisis.

On January 1, 2009, we were running out of cash quickly, but I wasn't worried since our investors still had $3 million earmarked to deploy as part of our Series A round. When we called that last tranche of funding, our investors refused because we had missed our sales target, causing us to default on our contract. Of course, we missed our target, I argued. Ninety-nine percent of companies missed their 2008 target. We had tripped one of their covenants. They were acting in bad faith, given that TAOS had grown 36 percent in 2008 over the previous year.

As a compromise, they proposed reevaluating our company based on current economic realities. Instead of $3 million at an $80 million valuation, they proposed to provide $300,000 at a $1 million valuation. Again, they were preying upon us, but this time, they wanted to take it all. In a not-so-diplomatic way, I refused. I immediately stopped paying interest on our loan to them, which was a very substantial quarterly amount. Our not-so-good relationship with our investors caused an all-out war.

Understanding I could not count on my investors, my team and I went into crisis management mode. We immediately took the following aggressive actions: a) stopped paying all interest to our investors, now our sworn enemies; b) stopped paying all rent, which caused us to default on more than forty leases we had worked so hard to acquire; c) reduced our inventory to a bare minimum, which allowed us to free up $1.5 million in cash; d) stopped all capex investments for new stores in the pipeline; and e) reduced head count. We were already running very lean, so we only let very few people go.

We were heading toward insolvency, so I consulted a bankruptcy lawyer to understand my options if we were forced to reorganize under chapter 11 protection, which is the bankruptcy code that generally provides for reorganization, involving a partnership or corporation. I kept that information to myself. I didn't even share it with Myriam to avoid causing her additional stress during her pregnancy.

In a few months, my spirit went from the highs of selling my company for a nine-figure amount to the gutter of facing insolvency and bankruptcy. Being an entrepreneur can feel like being on a roller coaster sometimes, but this felt like being thrown out of an airplane without a parachute. Thank goodness I could keep a cool head under that insane amount of pressure.

On the inside, though, my anxiety level was at an all-time high.

CHAPTER 19

The Art of the Deal

"Closing a deal is not an end; it's the beginning of a relationship."

—Unknown

In February 2009, at the height of my despair, while Myriam had an ultrasound at her OB-GYN in the other room, I called her cousin Michael, in London. He was Morgan Stanley's global chairman of M&A, representing some of Europe's most significant M&A deals of the past twenty years. I had met him the previous summer in Corsica, France, while attending a family wedding. In casual conversations, he had inquired if anyone had approached us to buy our company, given all our success. I couldn't share with him how deep in negotiations we were with P&G. Instead, I said that we were in early-stage dialogues with various groups.

I gave him a high-level explanation of the situation we found ourselves in and asked if he could provide some guidance. He offered better than that. He explained that he had recently retired from Morgan Stanley and was waiting out his noncompete period. He said he would be delighted to help me with this transaction since his noncompete allowed him to represent smaller clients like us. We agreed to collaborate.

At that moment, I felt grateful and hopeful for the luck I had with having someone of his caliber on my team. Moreover, he was family and a TAOS customer, and we were his only client then.

We went to work immediately to strategize how to get the P&G deal back on track. But first, I had to fire Goldman. They screwed up my deal not once but twice, and I wasn't about to let them do it a third time. My agreement with Goldman stated that they would get paid their commission if I sold the company within eighteen months after the termination of their contract. I negotiated a release from Goldman under the condition that I pay them a reduced fee of $900,000 should the sale to P&G go through.

Next, my new banker, Michael, prepped me for a face-to-face meeting with P&G's group president. I went up to Boston to have dinner with him. He and I had an excellent rapport. He immediately expressed P&G's admiration for TAOS and how Goldman had botched the process. "I kick myself. I knew we should have made a deal on the back of a napkin a year ago when we first spoke of this acquisition without bringing bankers into it. Bankers always screw things up," he said. "I agree," I replied, "but this is all new to me. Lesson learned." By the end of the evening, we agreed to resume the process and try to get this deal wrapped up quickly.

That was music to my ears.

With a great banker on my team, Goldman out of the way, and P&G back in the game, I felt I had an excellent chance to get this deal done and out of the mess I was in.

A funny thing happened the first time I introduced my new banker to P&G's M&A team on a conference call. When they heard his name, they immediately knew it was the same last name as my wife. They asked if he was related to Myriam. He replied, "Yes, Myriam's father is my first cousin." They must have thought I was the most desperate founder they had ever dealt with. Firing Goldman Sachs and hiring my wife's cousin sounded highly amateurish. Later, they must have googled him because they were behaving like groupies meeting a rock star on our second call together.

Meanwhile, Merrill Lynch, with whom we had a line of credit, was acquired by Bank of America (BoA) for pennies on the dollar. BoA started putting intense pressure on me to repay our line of credit, which we had been working with for the past nine years. I couldn't believe they were turning their back on us in this challenging time. I pleaded with them to give me just a couple of months to repay the line of credit in full, sharing P&G's official written offer to buy our company. I even proved to them I had enough funds in my personal account to repay the loan in the worst-case scenario that the P&G deal didn't go through. They wouldn't budge. Banks and their employees were in survival mode during this time. BoA started foreclosing on our loan.

P&G had yet to learn we had significant cash flow issues. They believed our investors had our back during this difficult time. But when they found out the bank was foreclosing on us, P&G's president contacted me to re-trade our deal.

The call went like this: "It has become clear that you are in a bad financial position, possibly facing insolvency. We could take advantage of the situation, but this is not how P&G likes to start relationships with founders we acquire. We pride ourselves in having good, long-term relationships with our founders before, during, and after acquisitions. But given the situation your company finds itself in, we must revise your valuation and our offer. We are willing to offer you $60 million instead of $80 million with 50 percent of the purchase price as an earnout period of eighteen months tied to delivering 22 percent sales growth." My heart sank. I didn't know what to say except, "OK, let me get back to you."

I did the math! If I sold for $60 million and missed getting my earnout after paying my investors and our debts, I would walk away with an amount I was not happy with. Going from a $180 million valuation down to a $80 million offer, down to $60 million was a tough pill to swallow.

The decision came down to whether or not I could achieve the earnout. Twenty-two percent sales growth in eighteen months was not easy to achieve but doable. The target numbers were measured against the trailing twelve months from June 2008 to May 2009, when sales had fallen 25 percent. We were also seeing that our sales were starting to rebound from the crisis and the stock market was beginning to show signs of recovery. I speculated that by Q4 2009, luxury retail would be back to normal. I was confident I could reach the target and get our earnout.

We owned an 82 percent stake in the company, meaning that most of the earnout would be paid to us. The only reason to reject the offer was to aspire to make more money if I sold my company to someone else in the future. This alternative was way too painful to think about. In bankruptcy proceedings, I would have to fight with my investors, bankers, and landlords. I could face losing my company. And who besides Gillette and P&G would want to buy a luxury shaving company? On the other hand, selling my company would give me freedom and well-being from not having all this stress.

Michael recommended I take the deal if I believed I could achieve my earnout. He told me it was a good deal. He had been in this situation many times and was less emotional than I was. He reminded me that although it was less than I wanted to sell the company for, it was still a lot of money. It was true, I thought, it was more money than I ever thought I would make in my life.

After weighing all options, I decided to take the deal and roll the dice.

A few days later, on March 2, 2009, Myriam gave birth to our first son. Eight days later, as is customary in the Jewish religion, we celebrated our son's circumcision with friends and family at our home in Miami Beach.

A week later, Michael met me in NYC to negotiate the final deal terms between the P&G team and our big city legal team. We sat in our lawyer's conference room all day to hash out every transaction detail. They agreed to increase the guaranteed portion of the purchase price to $35 million and reduce the earnout (a provision where the seller receives additional payments based on the company's future performance) to $25 million.

They also agreed to pay me a very generous salary plus a $1 million bonus if I stayed in my position until the end of the eighteen-month contract. Myriam was also well compensated for her consulting arrangement with P&G's research and development department. We shook on it. It was now in the hands of lawyers to draft all final closing documents and get us to the finish line.

Back in Miami, I had to turn around the situation with all my landlords for this deal to close. A few years earlier, we had charmed mall owners into giving us space in their centers. Then I defaulted on all our leases and now I promised to pay back all our unpaid rent and ask them to transfer all our leases to P&G. They all agreed, knowing that this was an excellent outcome for them. This was a sign of the times. These landlords would not have been this understanding in typical economic climates. I asked them to take my little unsecured company off the lease and replace it with one of the world's largest companies—a no-brainer from their perspective.

My greedy investors started tallying how much they were making on this deal. They tried to grab as much money as they could, and even made some basic math errors in their favor. We caught each mistake and kept them honest to the end. A few days before closing our transaction, they tried to bully us into paying them more money, threatening not to sign the deal if we disagreed. I knew wholeheartedly that they were bluffing, so I held my ground. I didn't believe they would walk away from this kind of payday in this economic environment with our relationship gone bad. I called each of their bluffs until thirty minutes before the final closing. Frankly, I could have done without this extra stress during that time.

On May 31, 2009, on a conference call, we closed our deal with P&G, and the funds were instantly wired to all the parties involved.

Our investors walked away with a 40 percent annualized return on their investment with TAOS—a good day at the office.

Michael called to congratulate me on closing this deal. He reminded me how incredible this achievement was and how impressed he was with the cool-headedness I showed during the past few challenging months. He complimented me, saying I had fought as bravely as some of the best clients he had witnessed over his long career.

It felt great to hear those words at that moment.

Our deal took fifteen grueling months to close. According to PricewaterhouseCoopers' report,[3] 2009 was one of the worst years for M&A transactions, with activity down 86 percent from the previous year. We were among the few deals that crossed the finish line that year. In the end, our company was bought for 2.2 times the revenue. Not bad for a company that had a negative earnings before interest, taxes, depreciation, and amortization (EBITDA), of -$500,000 per month during the final eight months of negotiations. The word profit was never discussed during the entire negotiation for TAOS sale. P&G allocated 95 percent of our purchase price to brand equity.

That is the difference between selling a brand versus selling a company. If my company were not a recognizable consumer brand name, it would have been worth much less, or dare I say nothing.

Valuation for recognized consumer brands differs significantly from that of successful companies. At the time of acquisition, a company can be valued for a multiple of EBITDA, usually in the range of three to ten times EBITDA. On the other hand, a reputable consumer brand can be valued for a multiple of sales.

To illustrate this point, we can use data from two publicly traded companies. Tesla, the best-selling electric vehicle manufacturer in the United States, sold 354,822 vehicles in the United States in 2022 with a market cap of $628 billion. In comparison, General Motors sold 5.9 million cars with a market cap of only $38 billion.[4] GM sold sixteen

3   Alexandra Zendrian, "M&A in 2009," July 14, 2009, https://www.forbes.com/2009/07/13/mergers-acquisitions-technology-intelligent-investing-healthcare.html?sh=24e9fb776e4f.

4   "Tesla Sales Figures—US Market," Good Car Bad Car, accessed April 9, 2024, https://www.goodcarbadcar.net/tesla-us-sales-figures/#:~:text=In%202022%2C%20Tesla%20sold%20a,with%20sales%20of%20195%2C447%20vehicles; Chris Isidore, "GM Shares Surge After Record Earnings and New Stake in Lithium Company," CNN Business, updated January 31, 2023, https://www.cnn.com/2023/01/31/investing/gm-earnings/index.html.

times more vehicles than Tesla for the same period, yet Tesla's market cap is sixteen times higher. Makes no sense! The easiest way to explain this is that investors pay for future potential more than current value. This example demonstrates the difference between the value of a hot, innovative brand with huge prospects versus an established company that sells many unexciting products.

Brands are so valuable because the odds of hitting one out of the park is very rare.

Minutes after closing our transaction, I laid down in my living room with my three-month-old baby boy sleeping in my arms. All the nerves in my body were pulsating, creating a tingling sensation under my skin.

It was the release of all the anxiety I had suppressed inside since the day P&G offered to buy our company.

I reminded myself my work wasn't done yet, as I still had to get our earnout.

A hard-won battle was behind me, but the war for our dreams was still raging.

CHAPTER 20

Integration and Earnout

"Most people fail in life not because they aim too high and miss, but because they aim too low and hit."

—Les Brown

Throughout the entire M&A process, only a handful of my employees were informed of our intentions to sell the business. We were acting on a need-to-know basis. The rest of the employees had no idea what was happening. It can be very disruptive if employees discover the company is being sold. Employees who hear their company is being sold can fear losing their job and seek other employment. Others may start speculating about the future and lose focus or motivation to perform their responsibilities.

The morning after we closed the transaction, on June 1, 2009, P&G executives, their integration team, Myriam, and I stood in front of all our local employees, with all our remote employees on a conference call to announce TAOS was acquired by P&G and Gillette. Some employees were stunned, some cried, and others cheered when they heard the news.

Ultimately, they were all reassured everyone's job was secure and that TAOS operations would go on as normal as possible. P&G had learned not to interfere too much with small companies they acquired, at least for the first few years. Our employees were also pleased to hear that I was asked to stay on as CEO and Myriam as a consultant for the company.

I felt I had done right by our employees, putting them in such good hands. Becoming a P&G employee through acquisition was an excellent opportunity for all our employees, as it is a great company to work for and offers notable benefits.

That afternoon, I immediately went to work on my earnout. I was not just hoping to make it; I was going to do everything in my power to make it. I wasn't going to let anything stand in our way of achieving the earnout. P&G executives were kind enough to make sure their integration team went out of their way to support us to achieve this goal. After all, they reasoned that if Myriam and Eric win, we win too.

The integration team was composed of a bunch of young up-and-comer executives looking to earn their stripes on small businesses like ours at the bottom of the P&G brand pyramid. The group leader was a young British guy I had worked with on the co-branded collaboration. I didn't think highly of his ability as a leader who could guide us to success, but I decided that he and I would keep a cordial rapport. The team also included a smart finance guy with whom I stayed in contact with years after the acquisition, as well as a brilliant young marketing executive who later became Dollar Shave Club's chief marketing officer. Myriam's position was replaced by a supply chain guy who played rugby in his free time. I felt that was an actual downgrade for the company, given Myriam's incredible talents in product development.

On the second day, I called a companywide sales meeting and explained our plan to deliver 50 percent growth within eighteen months. They thought I was crazy and pushed back but they knew I liked aiming high. I explained that we were up against meager numbers from sales that had dropped 25 percent over the previous twelve months and that the economy was rebounding. Plus we now had the largest marketing budget we had ever had to promote TAOS.

They got the message.

My management team and I began to plan a detailed strategy to increase our sales and reach our targets.

First, we reinstated our sales process, which had been neglected for the past few years. This retail sales process was designed to maximize the sales output of each associate in our stores. This was done by tracking specific key performance indicators (KPIs) and managing our sales team to the store averages of those KPIs. When we first introduced the process in 2002, we had seen a 20 percent lift in sales within months. Now, I estimated conservatively that it would give a 10 percent lift or more. Peter Drucker, the management guru, famously said, "What gets measured gets managed." The basic concept is that if you're measuring something, then the probability of you acting on the information you now have is a lot higher.

Second, I asked Gillette if we could offer all their blades in our stores. They were surprised by the request since they thought blades were a mass-market product and we were a luxury establishment. I respectfully explained that the blades are sold in mass-market channels but are a premium product at $25 for four blades. They agreed, and I treated blades like McDonald's treats fries. We instructed our staff to offer blades to every customer who made a purchase. "Would you like some blades with that?" We saw an immediate 6 percent sales lift from that initiative.

Third, we worked closely with our marketing team on deploying the new marketing budget we now had, to drive more traffic to our stores and website. This was the first time we had marketing budgets of that magnitude to work with. One of the many initiatives was to run ads in NYC subway carts and stations for a month. It was incredible to see our brand plastered all over town. The same town I had arrived in twenty-five years earlier.

P&G adopted a marketing campaign theme called "The Brotherhood." Myriam and I didn't like it at all. It felt too old-fashioned. Given its already very traditional products and image, we believed the brand needed to be modernized. Regardless, after giving our opinion, we followed the plan, knowing it would not affect the brand until we were long gone.

With P&G as my sugar daddy, we launched an initiative Myriam and I had dreamed of for a long time, but didn't have the budget for: redesigning our store's interiors.

We met with Gillette's management team and painted a picture of what TAOS 2.0 could look like. They loved the vision and gave us the green light to retrofit one store as a test. This initiative wasn't meant to help with our earnout since the impact of the retrofits would be realized well after we were gone. Nevertheless, we wanted to leave a legacy behind for the brand we had created in our Chelsea kitchen twelve years earlier. We wanted to leave TAOS with P&G better than they had found it at acquisition.

The redesign was a considerable success both aesthetically as well as revenue-wise. P&G approved the budget to retrofit all existing stores while new stores were built in the updated format.

At the time we were acquired, we had forty stores in operation. By the time we left the company in late 2010, the company had leases for almost one hundred stores. At its peak in 2014, TAOS operated 145 stores across the United States, generating over $100 million in revenue.

At the end of the eighteen-month integration period, we delivered 35 percent top-line growth, achieving 100 percent of our earnout. P&G was very pleased. I was ecstatic, but to say I was relieved would be an understatement.

Looking back on the last eighteen months at TAOS, I recognized that I had done some of my best work leading the company. After reflecting on it, I realized that this was because I was operating without all the usual stress I used to have as a CEO and founder, and I was left to do what I do best: lead strategy and growth. I realized how stress can impair our ability to perform our entrepreneurial duties at the highest level possible.

I used the analogy of swimming with a metal armor for all these years, and now I was swimming fast and easy in a speedo bathing suit. From the beginning, I ran the company with limited experience, limited resources, and a tremendous amount of stress on my shoulders.

Being an entrepreneur means operating under high pressure with significant responsibilities and high stress, which can impair cognitive abilities, decision-making skills, and overall performance. CEOs under such stress may have difficulty focusing, which can lead to emotional exhaustion, irritability, and mood swings. Can you relate to this?

That is the reason I believe a CEO's physical and mental well-being is essential to their ability to handle the demands of their role and to achieve long-term success. I wish I understood these factors when I started out.

One day, as I sat in a closed-strategy meeting with Gillette's top fifteen executives, I felt a sense of great pride. I had achieved something to be sitting in that room. A guy like me would never have had the opportunity to aspire to join P&G's management circle under normal circumstances. The eighteen months I worked inside P&G and the two years before that as a licensee have taught me invaluable business lessons that brought corporate structure and disciplines to my entrepreneurial habits and mindset.

Toward the end of our earnout period, P&G offered me to join the company full time with a generous salary package. I was flattered and grateful for the opportunity but respectfully declined the offer.

In hindsight, taking the offer may have been a good idea. It could have eased my transition post-exit. But I was in a different mindset at the time. I wanted to leave all of it behind. After all, that is why I wanted to sell my business in the first place. It was not to get a job working in corporate America. P&G showed me that it was an excellent company to work for. They are very respectful and generous with their employees. However, taking the position, I believe, would have broken my entrepreneurial spirit and creativity.

On Friday, December 10, 2010, I sent a heartfelt goodbye letter to all our employees. Later that afternoon, with every employee present in person or on a conference call, Myriam and I said our emotional goodbyes to our team. We thanked them and P&G for everything they did to help create this company. None of it would have been possible without each and every one of them.

We left our Doral, Florida, offices for the last time.

Four days later, Myriam gave birth to our second son.

Again, the timing was perfect.

TAOS redesigned store 2010

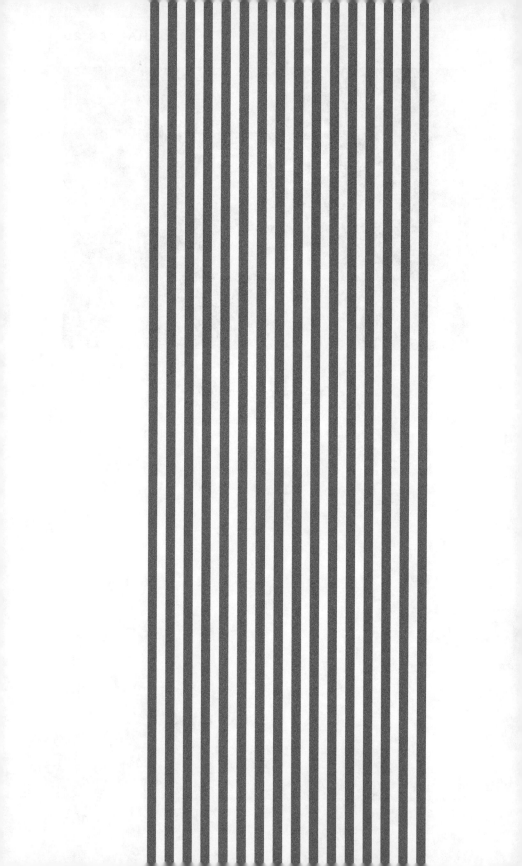

CHAPTER 21

The Great Unknown

"I'm not afraid of the unknown. I'm afraid of the known coming to an end."

—Morgan Freeman

On January 1, 2011, I woke up in a daze in our Miami Beach condo. My head was still spinning from the wild ride Myriam and I had been on for fourteen years. The ride came to a screeching halt when I heard our baby cry from the other room.

From the onset, TAOS afforded us a very comfortable lifestyle despite having no savings. It is common for entrepreneurs to reinvest all their cash back into the business after covering their expenses. After selling our company, our liquidity event didn't change our lifestyle much. The main difference was that we didn't have to worry about operating our business. I didn't feel the need to return to work, which was good because I didn't have the faintest idea of what I wanted to do next professionally.

I checked my agenda; it was clear for the next ten years. I realized at that moment that the universe gave me a gift, a unique opportunity to be 100 percent present for my kids' developmental years.

I felt fortunate for so many beautiful things in my life, including my wife, children, home, family, friends, and financial freedom. Nevertheless, transitioning from running an exciting company to being an at-home parent was challenging. I described my situation to friends like this: "I went from kicking ass to wiping ass."

At forty-one years old, I had achieved all the life dreams and aspirations I had set for myself. I was very grateful for the blessings in my life, but inside, I felt fearful, anxious, and unhappy. I realized then that nothing I could ever achieve would fill the void I had felt deep inside me for most of my life. Like many people, I thought, "When I sell my company, I will not be stressed anymore," and "When I have money, I will be happy." But that wasn't the case.

I realized my angst was an internal issue that had to be fixed from the inside out.

I reflected on my new life priorities for the journey ahead of me. My first priority was to be present as a father to my two sons. My second priority was to focus on my physical and mental health, and my third priority was to manage our family's assets.

My kids will always be my top priority. During the first ten years of their lives, which are a crucial time in a person's lifelong development, both Myriam and I were 100 percent present at all times. We focused on other priorities only while they were in school or day camp. Being stay-at-home parents was a unique situation for us and the kids. As always, Myriam and I were partners, and parenting was no different. We put our kids to bed, alternating between the boys each night unless they had a special request. We both changed diapers, fed them except breastfeeding, which was strictly Myriam's job, took them to the park, etc. We alternated school drop-offs and pick-ups. We both attended parent-teacher conferences and most doctor's visits.

I felt a sense of purpose that life had allowed me to be all in with my kids. This was especially meaningful since my father had not been there for me. Being a good father was healing for me in many ways. From the beginning of our relationship, Myriam and I instinctively knew that having kids and pursuing our career goals were incompatible. We were together for fourteen years before having our first child. I wanted to be financially secure before having kids so they wouldn't have to face the financial burdens I faced as a child. Having kids at forty-one allowed me to be more mature when I became a parent. Everyone is different, but for me, this was the perfect age to become a father.

Being clear about your priorities in life is essential for decision-making, and ultimately helps you allocate your time and energy on what's most important to you. It can allow you to let go of less important tasks and concentrate on what truly matters, minimizing the risk of spreading yourself too thin by pursuing too many things simultaneously.

When you are clear about your priorities, you can channel your efforts toward activities that contribute the most to your personal and professional growth. This enables you to set goals that align with your values, regardless of how unpredictable life can be. Whether it's planning your career, finances, or personal development, streamlining your priorities helps you set a realistic and meaningful path for the future.

Professionally, I had to dig deep to figure out what I wanted to do with life after TAOS. My ambitions had driven me obsessively in the past. Now that I had achieved my career and financial goals, I felt the fire in my belly dissolve. With all the time and resources on my hands, the options were limitless, confusing me more about what I wanted to do going forward.

It would have been great if I had a crystal ball to show me what the future had in store. But what fun would that be? The next best thing I found was the belief in the power of visualization to manifest things in our lives. Every five years, I write down the goals I want to achieve in my personal, professional, and family life. I do the same each calendar year. The more precise we are about what we want to manifest in our lives, the more likely it will be realized the way we want. Being too vague with our goals leaves room for surprises.

I tried to be very thoughtful about each goal I set to avoid being a victim of the saying, "Beware of what you wish for." I categorized my goals in three priorities of life: family, personal, and career. At the top of the page were my initials and the date. Below that I wrote the date five years from then. Below that, I wrote the age I would be in five years to get me in the planning mindset of thinking with the end in mind.

Keeping the end in mind, a principle rooted in strategic planning and personal development, prompts individuals to define long-term goals and envision success. By breaking down goals, prioritizing tasks, and aligning with values, this proactive approach fosters adaptability, effective time management, and a sense of purpose, as advocated in Stephen Covey's *The 7 Habits of Highly Effective People*.

In 2017, for my five-year plan, I wrote down ten goals I wanted to achieve by the end of 2022. Once finalized, I closed the document on my computer and filed it away. I rarely looked at them again for the next five years.

When I checked in on my goals early in 2022, I had achieved eight out of ten goals on my plan. I thought 80 percent was pretty good. The two remaining goals were achievable but unlikely before

2022. Believe it or not, one of those two remaining goals fell on my lap in May 2022. The final goal, an important deal I had been working on for years, came to a head in July and closed in November 2022, a month before the five-year plan deadline. I could hardly believe all ten goals I set five years earlier had been achieved. I truly feel the power of manifestation had something to do with it.

Give it a try! Write your goals clearly and thoughtfully, and see if they manifest.

CHAPTER 22

The Art of Investing

"Be willing to be uncomfortable. Be comfortable being uncomfortable. It may get tough, but it's a small price for living a dream."

—Peter McWilliams

The sale of TAOS was a life-changing event for our family. I had dreamed of being in this position my whole life, but like many entrepreneurs who achieved liquidity events, I wasn't prepared to manage investments.

I reached out to my CPA, who is well connected in our community. After assessing my situation, he recommended a wealth management team at BNY Mellon Bank. He explained that these guys won't achieve results better than other wealth managers, but they are honest and transparent with their fees. I took his recommendation and hired the team to manage some of our assets. They put together a classic stocks and bonds portfolio made up of eighty-plus different publicly traded companies. Their 1 percent fees of total assets under management would be charged whether my portfolio value went up or down. I thought that arrangement didn't align with my interest as a client, but I understood it was an industry standard.

I met with my bankers quarterly to review our portfolio with impressive graphs and charts they had prepared. At first, I tried to keep up with the conversation about economic fundamentals, asset allocation, time horizon, and diversification.

The first time my portfolio experienced a 20 percent drop in value due to a market correction, the banker called me immediately to reassure me about the economy and to stay the course of our investments. I didn't realize at the time that keeping clients from selling stock in a market panic is one of the most significant values wealth managers provide their clients.

After eighteen months of working with BNY Mellon, I noticed they only made a few trades on my account annually. What they did didn't seem very complicated. They picked stocks, many of which I recognized, and held them for extended periods. Meanwhile, very high amounts of money were being withdrawn from my account each month to cover their management fees.

I started getting an itch to control and manage my assets. But it sounded a bit wild to think I could do that. After all, I had no financial training or formal education in this area.

After selling our business, there were three things that became very clear to me. The first was that at forty-three, I felt I was way too young to retire. Truthfully, I am still trying to figure out if I will ever be old enough to retire. The second was that I also knew that I no longer wanted to have the stress I had experienced when running my business. I wanted an occupation that added value to society and one that I was passionate about. And third, I wanted to generate enough passive income from our investments to live on for the rest of our lives. This meant having all my expenses covered by the returns of our investments.

While wondering what I wanted to do professionally in the future, I realized I had a critical mission on my hands: to manage our family's assets. This was my most crucial responsibility in my professional life, and I needed to make it my focus. To handle this responsibility, I only had two choices: outsource the management of our assets to professionals or manage it on my own. I had no other occupations in front of me, and since I was very excited about the prospect of becoming an investor, I decided to develop our own family office. Hence, I promoted myself to chief investment officer of our family office.

The first item on my to-do list was learning The Art of Investing.

I approached investing as I approached my business, and started by writing a business plan. I am a fan of Sun Tzu's philosophy of winning the war before it is fought, coincidentally named The Art of War.

I asked myself: *What is my purpose? What is my goal? What is my strategy? What do I want? What do I need to do to get what I want?*

These are simple questions to ask but difficult to answer.

Years later, I would learn that the business plan I was developing was called an Investment Policy Statement. This document is usually drafted between a portfolio manager and a client, outlining the manager's mandate. This statement states a client's general investment goals and objectives and describes the strategies the manager should employ to meet these objectives. I assumed the manager role in this case, and my family was the client.

To develop this business plan, I first had to decide if I was a defensive or enterprising investor, as defined by Benjamin Graham in his book *The Intelligent Investor*. The defensive investor's goal is to avoid losses and generate a decent return while minimizing the time he spends managing his portfolio while pursuing other activities.

On the other hand, the enterprising investor devotes more time and effort to researching securities, hoping to make a better average return than the passive investor over the long term. The difference is less about taking more risks than it is about making this your full-time work. The enterprising investor must know about the stock market and make this a full-time business.

I decided on a hybrid model called a barbell strategy, an investment or risk management approach that involves concentrating resources on two extreme ends of a spectrum while avoiding the middle. The process involves allocating investments in low-risk, conservative assets on one end, and high-risk, potentially high-reward holdings on the other. The goal is to achieve a balance that provides stability and security on one side while allowing for potential growth and returns on the other.

The barbell strategy is designed to protect against the potential downsides of both extremes. The conservative assets provide stability and a hedge against market volatility, while the high-risk investments offer the potential for substantial gains.

I decided to invest 80 percent of my assets as a defensive investor in stocks, bonds, and real estate investments and spend 20 percent of my time managing them. For the remaining 20 percent portion of our assets, I wanted to invest in private companies within my industry; I would be an enterprising investor 80 percent of my time.

For the rest of my reflection, I landed on the following:

Our objective is to ensure financial security during our lifetime and beyond, enjoy life to the fullest, provide our children with an excellent education, and help those in need.

Our goal was to achieve an average rate of return of 8 to 10 percent annually on our assets, which is easier said than done.

The strategy we adopted to reach our goal was to invest most of our capital in Exchange Traded Funds (ETFs) to create a diversified portfolio of stocks and bonds with low management fees that are tax efficient. I allocated 65 percent to US equities and 35 percent to international equities.

To further diversify and increase our average rate of return, we would invest in private equity funds specializing in real estate and others in consumer goods. However, the key to successful long-term wealth preservation is to manage and control spending so that it is no more than 3 to 4 percent of total assets annually.

For the entrepreneurial side of our portfolio, we created a private investment fund called Strategic Brand Investments (SBI) that would take higher risks with the potential for higher returns. This fund would invest in early-stage entrepreneurs for whom our business and industry experience could make a big difference.

So, I embarked on a new journey of learning how to become an investor. I started reading books about investing to study the recommendations of some of the greatest investors of our time. I was pleasantly surprised that most books demystified the notion that an investor like me needed a wealth manager to be successful. This reinforced my own bias, so I wasn't entirely convinced it was that easy to pull off.

The authors echoed the wisdom to invest long term in a low-cost, tax-efficient, diversified portfolio with an asset allocation risk profile you are comfortable with. The information that hit home for me was that less than 10 percent of active wealth managers outperform the stock market. The main reason is the wealth managers' hefty annual fees on your assets. When compounded over the long term,

1 to 1.5 percent fees can add up to 40 percent or more of your total portfolio returns. The information started to confirm what my gut was telling me.

I *can* and *must* manage our investments.

Research shows that the industry's most significant investor pitfall is what is known as "investor psychology, and the belief that we can time the market." We all know the adage to buy low and sell high, but in reality, many amateur investors fall victim to the opposite. When the market corrects or crashes regularly, and fear sets into the markets with media sound bites that scream, "*SELL SELL SELL before it's too late,*" many investors sell stocks to minimize the damage. They then miss the market rally on the way up and lose.

Fear and greed are the two emotions that drive most investors' psychology. Managing this investor psychology, I realized, was the most significant challenge for an investor like me. I believed I had the temperament to be a disciplined investor. Still, I also knew that my family's loss of fortune during my teenage years and the fact that we almost went into bankruptcy during the sale of our company to P&G would work against me.

The other challenge I realized was that I needed to transition my mindset from the entrepreneurial headspace to that of an investor's. Entrepreneurs are trained to think and focus on short-term business goals and challenges. That had been my mindset during my entire career thus far. The investor mindset, however, requires poise and patience to succeed. The time horizon of an investor can define his entire strategy. As Warren Buffett cleverly said, "Money is transferred from the impatient to the patient." I knew from having raised money for my previous business that VCs expect a return on their investment within seven to ten years. That can feel like a long wait for an entrepreneur or untrained investor.

I still needed more knowledge, confidence, and expertise to become a full-fledged investor.

Coincidentally, I received an advertising mailer that promoted a wealth management course at the University of Chicago. I usually discarded these types of promotional mail, but this one caught my attention. I researched it online and found that I fit the exact target audience this course was catering to. The cost was a hefty $10,000 plus travel expenses to attend in person, and I had to prove I had sufficient net worth to be accepted to take the course. It looked legitimate, so I decided to lean in and sign up.

I attended the four-day course in October 2014. The university pavilion and the course faculty were imposing. The small class of forty students was made up of people from different countries and different ages. Some were first-generation wealth creators like myself; others were fifth-generation heirs in training to start managing their family's assets.

I returned from the course with the confidence and the know-how I needed to create and manage our investment portfolio. I felt ready to set up and manage our small family office.

One of the most exciting lessons I learned there as an investor is the relationship between risk and reward. This concept is at the core of all investing decisions. The risk-reward ratio is a calculation used by investors to measure the potential gains of an investment against the risk of loss.

The higher the risk you take, the higher the potential for reward there should be for you. Inversely, the lower the risk, the lower the reward. For example, Treasury Bills guaranteed by the US government with zero risk provide the lowest interest available. Therefore, entrepreneurs who set their goals extremely high with a very low probability of success are the ones who stand to gain the most if they beat the odds. An entrepreneur with a reasonable goal of creating a business that supports a decent lifestyle is more likely to achieve his target; therefore, the reward is lesser.

Have you ever gambled in a casino? You get paid thirty-six times your bet at the roulette table because you have a one in thirty-six chance to win, whereas you get paid two times your bet if you get it right between black and red, which has a fifty-fifty chance to win.

A relationship between risk and reward can also help us make smaller decisions in life. For example, deciding to go skydiving can be viewed as a risk-reward relationship. Jumping out of an airplane with a parachute is relatively safe nowadays (low risk). The idea of skydiving sounds excellent to you (high reward). Then it would be best to go skydiving because it's low risk and a high reward. If skydiving, on the other hand, sounds horrible to you, then it might fall in the category of high risk with low reward. Therefore, you shouldn't do it. We all make unconscious risk-reward decisions every day of our lives.

Initially, I retained my bankers to manage their portfolios while I started deploying a separate portfolio with funds I had on the sidelines. A year later, I terminated my relationship with my bankers and moved all assets to our self-managed account.

A few friends who knew what I was doing thought I was making a grave mistake. That added to the pressure and doubt I was already feeling. I was scared, but I reminded myself of the great minds that I studied at the University of Chicago. I remembered the books I read by Warren Buffet, Benjamin Graham, and others who prescribed these lessons and assured me, in their writing, that I was doing the right thing as long as I respected the true and tested principles in investing.

My experiences with M&A, raising angel capital and venture capital, and selling TAOS inspired me to become an angel investor by investing in up-and-coming entrepreneurs in my industry. This is where I would invest a small part of our assets to be an active, enterprising investor.

In 2014, we found our first opportunity for SBI to invest in a skincare business through our local South Florida network. The company had an interesting business model that fit well within our expertise and they needed a lot of work to get on track, but it was profitable and cash-positive. We decided to invest and take a minority stake of 30 percent in the company. Myriam and I rolled up our sleeves and went to work helping our new partners develop their company.

That experience was very fulfilling for me. I realized that helping entrepreneurs achieve their goals is what I wanted to do professionally. Even more encouraging, in 2022, we exited that investment, generating a ten-time return on our investment. This was a massive win for SBI.

The success of this investment gave me the experience and the success I needed to pursue my dream of becoming an angel investor.

After the crash of 2008, the stock market experienced one of the most significant bull markets in history. During the early years of managing my portfolio independently, I made various mistakes I had been taught to avoid. Those mistakes were precious in my training to become an investor and I justified those errors as part of my learning curve. For the five years between 2019 and 2023, I started to get my stride as an investor and achieved an annual investment return of 8 percent.

When markets were rattled during the pandemic between 2019 and 2022, I was able to navigate the rough waters without panicking. That grew my confidence and made me feel like I was starting to develop the right mindset for the job. I aim to continue improving my skills and strategies to reach or exceed my target return goals in the future.

Interestingly, the small portfolio I manage for my two boys with the same approach generated 11 percent annually during the past ten years. That illustrates that investor psychology plays a vital role in your risk tolerance and, therefore, in your investment returns.

Our life experiences, upbringing, education, and community cause us to develop biases. Biases are a disproportionate weight in favor of or against an idea or thing, and can be innate or learned, good or bad. These biases unconsciously drive many of our decisions in life and business. Suppose you are not aware of your own biases. In that case, you can fall victim to "confirmation bias," which is a tendency for people to favor information that confirms their beliefs while ignoring information that goes against them. Another way to think of this is "wishful thinking," which is an attitude or confidence that something you want to happen will happen even though it is not likely or possible. This can lead to many errors in judgment and poor decisions. When you add what is called "noise" to bias, it can turbocharge your poor choices. Noise can be described as external information that feeds your biases and can come from many different sources, including friends, the media, algorithm-targeted social media messages, books, and the collective actions of others.

Warren Buffett once said, "It's wise for investors to be fearful when others are greedy and to be greedy only when others are fearful." To achieve this unconventional mindset, one must have the courage to think for oneself and cut out the noise around them that feeds the biases. As an investor, I was encouraged not to look at my investment statements frequently and to avoid watching financial media news.

To illustrate this example, if you believe that owning a home is always better than renting one (your bias), then when you hear messages that the real estate market is booming and you should get in on the action before it goes up again (noise), this can lead you to buy a home at the top of the market, which is not always ideal.

The primary way to ensure you don't fall victim to noise and bias is by making sure to avoid on-the-fly decisions. You should also learn to be open-minded. To do this, you should methodically evaluate decisions so you can analyze both sides of the judgment with extreme open-mindedness.

Most importantly, to be a successful investor, you must train yourself to be comfortable with being uncomfortable.

CHAPTER 23

What's Inside Matters Most

Early on, Myriam and I understood that artificial chemicals are harmful to humans and should be avoided as much as possible. But it wasn't until 2018 that we made a mind-boggling discovery. All artificial chemicals are made from petroleum. Let me repeat that: all artificial chemicals are made from petroleum, also known as petrochemicals.

So, what is a petrochemical?

Petrochemicals are the chemical products obtained from refining petroleum. Some chemical compounds from oil are also obtained from other fossil fuels, such as coal or natural gas, or renewable sources, such as maize, palm fruit, or sugarcane. Petrochemical products are used to make thousands of products in everyday life, including plastics, rubbers, resins, synthetic fibers, adhesives, dyes, detergents, pesticides, petroleum-derived paints, coatings, fragrances, and many other things. Petrochemical products are everywhere, exposing us to dangerous chemicals that threaten our health. Even the food wax coating on many fruits and vegetables, such as bell peppers, potatoes, and cucumbers, is produced from petrochemicals. Food coloring also derives from petrochemicals, so any foodstuff with artificial pigmentation will contain them.

Did you know that 99 percent of pharmaceuticals are made with petrochemical raw materials? Common petrochemicals used include various solvents, reagents, and building blocks in the synthesis of drug compounds. This includes over-the-counter (OTC) medication, prescription drugs, and medicine such as antihistamines, antibacterial, suppositories, cough syrups, lubricants, creams, ointments, salves, analgesics, and hand sanitizers. Most people are surprised to hear this for the first time.

Did you know all synthetic fibers like nylon and polyester are made from petroleum? This means yoga pants, exercise shorts, bathing suits, dresses, pants, shirts, and baby clothes are made of petroleum. Yes, nowadays, most clothes we wear are made of or contain synthetic fibers. If you don't believe me, check the labels and google the fabric names.

The beauty industry is not as pretty as they make themselves out to be either. Most personal care products, including skin care, body care, hair care, and makeup, are filled with petrochemicals. Over 10,000 chemicals make their way to unsuspecting consumers inside billions of personal care products annually.

There is no way to avoid chemicals in modern societies but you can limit your contact with them if you become more aware of their existence.

This is a glaring blind spot in our society.

Throughout our more than twenty-five-year career in the beauty industry, Myriam and I became aware of industry-wide practices we disagreed with. Most alarming were all the toxic ingredients used in personal care products. Every day, the average person comes into contact with hundreds of harmful chemicals found in these products. We strongly believe that synthetic chemicals are responsible for many women's health issues.

We also noticed that the average skin care product contained thirty to eighty ingredients diluted in 50–80 percent water. As a green formulator, Myriam knew that a product containing too many ingredients would give you a microdose of each, rendering the effectiveness of each component virtually useless, delivering no efficacy. To add insult to injury, consumers were duped into paying hundreds of dollars for these products.

Another aspect of the beauty industry we didn't appreciate was that brands made consumers believe that men's and women's products differed and that different moisturizers worked on different skin types. Hair care companies make us think this shampoo is for redheads and this one's for curly hair. Meanwhile, we knew the only difference between any of those products was, in most cases, packaging and fragrance.

What infuriated us most was that the ingredients were hidden on the back of the packaging, written in tiny fonts you couldn't read without a magnifying glass. Even if you could read them, you would not understand what the complicated chemical names were.

Sustainability became a trendy word. Brands made with synthetic chemicals packaged in plastic bottles promoted themselves as environmentally friendly. That felt wrong to us!

During the 2010s, as the clean beauty movement started to pick up steam with consumers, we saw a wave of greenwashing brands getting in on the action. Greenwashing is the act of making false or misleading statements about the environmental benefits of a product or practice by claiming they were natural when, in fact, they were not.

Natural ingredients were already a critical philosophy for us with TAOS products. Shortly after leaving TAOS in 2011, Myriam and I began brainstorming about the ideal personal care brand—a brand whose products we would want to buy for ourselves and our children. We imagined a brand that would be formulated with the purest and highest-quality organic ingredients, free of petrochemicals.

The brand's purpose would be focused on consumer health and wellness instead of corporate interest. Most importantly, it would bring ingredients into focus instead of being hidden in tiny fonts on the back of the packaging. As we brainstormed the idea, we thought we should feature the list of ingredients in large fonts on the front of the bottles. We both loved the idea of bringing ingredients to the forefront of the brand.

The more we talked about this brand, the more we realized we have always been obsessive about everything that goes into our products. So much so that we thought we could name this new brand after what's inside—Ingredients®.

We loved the idea!

In 2011, right after leaving TAOS, we had no intentions of creating or launching a new brand, but we were so excited about the name that we decided to apply for the Ingredients® trademark with the US Patent and Trademark Office. One year after we applied, the Ingredients® trademark was accepted.

We were very excited about securing the trademark, but we went on with our lives.

Fast-forward to December 2018. Myriam had just completed a big product formulation project she was working on. She felt it was time for her to create the brand we had imagined eight years before.

At first, I resisted the idea of launching a new start-up. I knew too well how much time and money would be required. But Myriam intended to disrupt the beauty industry with a product line like no other. By this point we were so intimate with the beauty industry that we were well aware of all the toxic ingredients in the majority of products that consumers couldn't see. Not just toxic ingredients but also a lack of transparency, high prices, and made-up marketing claims packaged in beautiful plastic bottles and fragranced with wonderful aromas made from chemicals.

In January 2019, we agreed to launch this new project. Myriam and I returned to our roots of building a start-up, and we gave it the fitting name, Ingredients®. People around us assumed that after our success with TAOS, we knew what we were doing. We now had more resources, connections, and business experience. But creating and scaling a new consumer brand is a new mountain to climb. As a young, scrappy entrepreneur thirty years earlier, I had much less experience, fewer resources, and connections, but I had hustle, grit, and no plan B. That was my edge.

Now, I had to find a new edge. This time, it was passion and purpose. It's hard to admit, but in hindsight, the first business was all about ME. This time, it was about giving back, adding value to others, and positively impacting society. We felt a duty to help protect the health of consumers.

For the next two years, Myriam developed some of the best formulas she had ever created. I could see improvements in her craft and science with each new product. Her formulation philosophy for our new brand was to use only eight ingredients or less per product.

Each of those ingredients would be active plant-based ingredients and organic whenever possible. This means we didn't use water to dilute our formulas. Instead, we used rose, neroli, and lavender plant waters, known as hydrosols. Myriam sourced the highest-quality ingredients from all the great producers we met worldwide during our careers.

Regarding packaging, as always, Myriam had a clear vision for this new product line. She wanted our bottles to look pharmaceutical and be environmentally friendly. She chose glass and post-recycled aluminum packaging.

By the time we started developing Ingredients®, the clean beauty revolution was already on the way. Clean is the term coined by the beauty industry for brands that make safer consumer formulas. Since the FDA doesn't regulate the beauty industry, brands can put almost any ingredients in their formulas and claim they are clean. Europe and Japan are much stricter when it comes to these regulations. Over 1,500 ingredients are banned in most countries, while only eleven are banned in America.

So many clean beauty brands were launching in the industry that we wondered how our new brand would cut through the noise and be noticed. To attract attention, we needed to do something that had never been done before. That is when we decided to be "radically transparent" by printing the ingredients and the exact percentages on the front of the bottles. This was an industry first.

We hired a fantastic boutique design firm in Toronto, Canada, to help us bring our new brand vision to life. When we described our vision, the design team became very excited. After all, they hear new brand pitches daily but had never heard anything like what we were presenting to them. They were incredibly amazed that we had secured a trademark for the word Ingredients. We collaborated creatively with our design firm, working closely with them as we always did with agencies. Ultimately, they created a beautiful brand design we were very excited about.

The most challenging part of the project was creating formulas that contained zero artificial chemicals, that is, petrochemicals. With this challenge came the pressure point of having product stability and achieving a three-year shelf life, usually accomplished using synthetic preservative systems like parabens or others. Myriam identified two new plant-based preservative systems she thought could work, but we weren't sure our goal could be achieved. After all, we had never seen a water-based skin care product made without synthetic preservatives. When water and oxygen meet, bacteria forms. We needed to find a lab experienced with these formulas to achieve our goal. We asked the ingredient manufacturer for lab clients who purchased these plant-based preservatives. They referred us to one of the best beauty manufacturers in the United States. Often, these large manufacturers don't take in small clients and have large minimum production requirements.

Nevertheless, we met with the manufacturer and pitched our new brand vision and philosophy. They, too, became very excited about our idea. They agreed to work with us and even reduced their minimum volume requirements to facilitate the start of our relationship. They explained they do this for only one or two exceptional new projects every year. We were encouraged to hear this and worked with their lab technicians immediately. Myriam provided them with formulas she had designed, samples she had made in our office, and each ingredient she had sourced for each formula. The lab helped us achieve a final formula and all the standard lab tests to ensure shelf life, packaging compatibility, and microbial safety. At first, some of the tests failed, but after adjusting the preservative system levels, we finally got the green light to go into production.

Less than one year into developing Ingredients, the pandemic started. The next thing we knew was that people were confined to their homes with little to no contact with the outside world except via Zoom, email, and phone. We used this limitation to our advantage. With no social and travel distractions, we obsessively dove into our work. From start to launch, this project took twenty-two months.

In November 2020, we started delivering our first products to customers, but the official launch wasn't until February 2021.

Our radical transparency strategy and our reputation as TAOS founders helped the new brand get recognized within the industry. We leveraged our beauty industry connections to launch the brand in over one hundred stores in the first nine months.

The excitement around the brand was encouraging; however, the e-commerce side of the business, which we had launched simultaneously, didn't perform well. We realized that the recent changes in privacy laws and our lack of digital marketing experience made this a challenging distribution channel for us to master.

Although I was very passionate about the brand's purpose, the day-to-day running of a new business started to feel more like a burden than a joy. I knew from experience that I needed three things to build a successful brand and company: time, motivation, and digital expertise. Unfortunately, I was lacking in all three.

I realized I didn't have the kind of hustle I had when I first started my career. I no longer had the time to dedicate to this project, as many other occupations required my focus. I had missed the e-commerce revolution of 2010–2020 and found myself lost in the new digital world of brand building. Our industry, consumers, and the world felt like a new planet I had never visited before.

I came to the difficult conclusion that someone other than me was the right person to run this company. I put my ego aside and reminded myself to stay open-minded because no two journeys are alike. I started shifting my mindset to reimagine how we could develop Ingredients.

Stay tuned. The road to success is always under construction.

CHAPTER 24

Angel Investing

So, if I didn't want to run a start-up ... what did I want to do?

This is the first question we should ask ourselves when thinking about our future. Sometimes, I even ask myself, "What would I say to someone if they were in my situation?" Taking the emotion out of the question makes me think clearly. An old Spanish proverb roughly translates to, "The cobbler's children have no shoes." This means someone with a specific skill is often so busy assisting others that their affairs go unattended.

To help me think about my answer in a methodological way, I again turned to Jim Collins and the "Hedgehog Concept" he developed for the book *Good to Great*. It is a simple, crystalline concept that flows from a deep understanding of the intersection of three circles: (1) what you are deeply passionate about, (2) what you can be the best in the world at, and (3) what best drives your economic or resource engine.

I dug deep again to tap into the wisdom of all the lessons I had learned during the past thirty years of my career.

What am I deeply passionate about?

I am deeply passionate about helping people. More specifically, in a professional context, I landed on helping the next generation of entrepreneurs achieve their goals using all my business and life experiences. It is something I have always found very fulfilling.

What can I be the best in the world at?

Over the years, I have mentored many entrepreneurs who often told me that my guidance made a huge difference in their lives, which made me believe I could be good at this. Investors think they provide entrepreneurs with strategic help, but in my experience, they primarily offer funding and introductions within their network. I could differentiate myself by being the piece young entrepreneurs need most: an experienced strategic partner who walks along with them during their journey.

Finally, what best drives your economic or resource engine?

If done right, investing in early-stage companies can be a great business model and financially lucrative. After all, I had already proven this point when I exited our first investment after seven years, for ten times our initial investment. By helping entrepreneurs achieve their goals, I could benefit from their success by having a minority stake in their company.

I had found my hedgehog to develop SBI into a full-fledged angel fund.

Now that I figured out what I wanted, I needed to figure out what steps I needed to take to achieve it.

First, an investor must be very clear about their target investment. The more disciplined an investor is, the better his fund will perform over the long term. In our case, the target investments needed to meet specific personal and business criteria. The top priority, we decided, was that the founder(s) we invest in must be coachable and open-minded. To be vetted, the entrepreneur must have personal references within my network. Investing in companies whose products are minimally toxic to human health and our planet is also significant to me personally. The final requirement was that the business must have a clear path to a scalable and profitable model.

My goal was to work with entrepreneurs who have already raised seed capital and brought their businesses to market but who still needed to raise professional funding. In my experience, between the family round and the venture round, entrepreneurs need more guidance than money. By then, they usually have proof of concept for their business model while mistakes and challenges have caught up to them. Maybe their growth had stalled, or sometimes they ran out of cash, or their business model was not profitable. Most importantly, they are at a stage when they know they need the help I can provide. With the right expertise and guidance, it is possible to bring their business to the point of becoming investable.

Our goal and how we differentiate ourselves from other investor groups is to invest in companies where our expertise and ongoing guidance can disproportionately impact the company's success.

I aim for SBI to develop a portfolio of unique brands by partnering with extraordinary founders. Being an entrepreneur or founder can be a lonely job and having a seasoned entrepreneur with a proven track record by your side can be a game changer. I could have used someone like that when I was on the front lines.

During my career, I learned many lessons about building and running a successful business. When I work with entrepreneurs, I can relate to their current situation and understand exactly how it feels to be in their shoes from having experienced it on my own journey. This is what differentiates me as an investor and as a business coach.

I dedicate myself to helping entrepreneurs achieve their goals by investing in their companies, mentoring them, and writing this book, a book I have written with these particular entrepreneurs in mind.

I hope that sharing the lessons I've learned in my journey will help you in your journey.

CHAPTER 25

Health Is Wealth

It was important for me to include a chapter about health in this book because, throughout my entrepreneurial journey, I've realized that health is not just a personal asset but also a business necessity. Overlooked by many entrepreneurs, optimal health is the foundation of success.

My discovery of holistic health, beginning in my early twenties, intertwined seamlessly with my entrepreneurial path, revealing my true calling: a synergy of entrepreneurship and wellness.

Myriam and I bonded by our mutual passion for natural living, found in our relationship as life partners and as business allies. Our shared commitment to a natural lifestyle has been the bedrock of our relationship and a driving force behind our entrepreneurial ventures.

When I was twelve, I began experiencing digestive issues and migraines after moving to Canada. They were so frequent that they became the norm, and I simply went on with life, ignoring the discomfort. Conventional medicine offered little relief. The only thing that helped was OTC medication like Alka Seltzer, which I renamed "Malka Seltzer" because I was taking them so often.

It was only through my foray into natural health in my twenties, inspired by a colleague's triumph over chronic arthritis through herbal remedies, that I began to understand the importance of addressing the root causes of illness. This epiphany set me on a path of discovery, adopting a diet rich in natural, unprocessed foods and holistic remedies.

Myriam's journey to a natural lifestyle also started at a very young age, rooted in the natural setting of her childhood on the outskirts of Paris, France. She, too, had health issues in her childhood that prompted her to become a vegetarian.

We define wellness as the active pursuit of optimal health. It is a lifestyle approach based on a holistic mindset. Wellness is a journey during which I have discovered the gift of nature and the hazards of chemical toxicity.

Wellness matters because every physical action we take and every emotion we feel as humans relates to our well-being; in turn, well-being directly affects our actions and emotions. Wellness is not simply the lack of suffering from disease but describes good mental and physical health.

A wellness-based approach addresses the root source of an ailment. Wellness practitioners take a holistic view of human biology to identify the factors causing symptoms (i.e., headache)—including diet, lifestyle, and environmental considerations—effectively preventing symptoms of illness rather than treating them.

In contrast, modern medicine is laser-focused on treating symptoms rather than treating the root cause. If a person has a headache, traditional medical doctors will present pharmaceutical solutions to alleviate the headache, disregarding the rest of human function.

Whenever possible, I use modern medicine for the available diagnostic tools. Once I understand the ailment, I first solve it with holistic remedies, leaving medication and surgeries as a last resort.

Over the past thirty years, this health philosophy has helped me heal medical issues with counter-instinctive methods. Here are some examples and personal anecdotes.

In 2005, Myriam saw a dermatologist to address spider veins in her legs. He offered to do twenty shots in two back-to-back sessions instead of over a few months, and Myriam didn't know any better, so she agreed. After completing the second round, Myriam went home and felt a shooting pain in her right knee. It was excruciating when she walked, but she thought it was just some kind of a strain. The next day, her left knee started hurting too. Within a few days, Myriam was not able to walk at all. It was a terrifying moment for us. We saw many doctors and received many different diagnostic and treatment recommendations, ranging from surgery to more injectables. The problem endured and months went by that Myriam could hardly get up from the couch. After several months of desperation, we returned to our natural roots and sought help from alternative doctors. Myriam made an appointment with a reputable Chinese doctor in Fort Lauderdale, Florida. While she was explaining her knee problem, the doctor took her arm, checked her pulse, and then went on to check her tongue, which is customary in Chinese medicine. The doctor could immediately tell that Myriam's kidneys were weak, operating at roughly only 20 percent of their capacity. She explained that, in Chinese medicine, the kidneys and the knees are directly related. If the kidneys are weak, so are the knees. Myriam told her about the injections she had recently received and wondered if that was the cause of her knee issues. Of course, the answer was yes. Her kidneys were overloaded with toxicity from the twenty injections, and her body had gone into shock, unable to function properly for more than six months. With this diagnosis in hand, Myriam started a strict detoxification process that included Chinese herbal medication. Little by little, her knees healed, and within a few months, both her kidneys and knees were back to normal. Myriam never experienced knee pain again. It was a traumatic experience reinforcing our belief in the human body as a profoundly complex, interdependent system.

In 2018, our son developed tics that caused his eyes to roll around uncontrollably. As parents, this was a terrifying thing to witness. After consulting various doctors, we decided to do our research. We found articles online that linked metal braces in teens to tics. Once we identified the problem, we asked our dentist to remove the metal spacer she had put in a few months prior. We believed the metal was reacting to Wi-Fi signals and devices throughout the home. After removing the metal from our son's mouth, the tics disappeared within forty-eight hours and were never an issue again.

In 2022, I started getting migraines again. So intense that they induced vomiting. At first, it happened every few months, and eventually, it happened once a week or more. I ran every test imaginable, but my doctor found nothing unusual. During the summer of 2023, we traveled for an entire month. During that time, I experienced none of the migraine symptoms I had been having when I was home. Within two days of my return home, I had a migraine and vomiting episode. I was convinced the house was making me sick. We bought home mold test kits and placed them throughout the house. Sure enough, our upstairs den had mold. We hired a mold remediation company that identified traces of mold in our AC units. Mold is prevalent in Florida but is often detected too late. We checked into a hotel for ten days during the remediation process. Since moving back into the house, I have never experienced my symptoms again.

My holistic training has taught me to deal with the source of the matter instead of what is showing up on the surface. In this case, instead of treating the migraine with medicine, I unveiled what was causing the migraines in the first place. The mindset that "doctor knows best" may be a bias in some cases.

Having an open mind means consulting a doctor and a holistic practitioner when facing medical issues, and from there you can get all the facts and make an educated decision for yourself.

Take baby steps to introduce new health habits into your lifestyle. At first, it will take some conscious effort, but in time, it will become second nature.

I am not a doctor, and this chapter is not meant to be medical advice but instead to be viewed as an invitation to explore natural health. It's about living vibrantly for as long as we are alive, not just prolonging life. My philosophy is preventative, focusing on lifestyle changes in the hope of avoiding common diseases that often curtail longevity. I base this philosophy on six health pillars: nutrition, hydration, sleep, breathing, fitness, and mental health.

Hippocrates, a famous Greek physician in 440 BC, traditionally referred to as the "Father of Medicine," said it best: "Let food be thy medicine and let thy medicine be food."

Eating and drinking are the foundation of human health. Indeed, our modern lifestyle has brought with it modern illness. Reducing toxicity and, with that, reducing inflammation is key. When we think about food, we know that through science, lower calorie diets (not to be confused with fat-free diets) are linked to longevity and lack of diseases. Yet, we live in a country where people eat like it's their last meal from morning to night, while ingesting harmful ingredients nonstop. Getting accustomed to eating less by either portion control or intermittent fasting can benefit humans tremendously.

My personal nutritional diet consists primarily of plant-based, alkaline foods such as organic vegetables, fruits, nuts, and seeds; organic proteins such as meat, chicken, fresh-caught fish, and legumes; and healthy fats such as olive, avocado, and coconut oils.

I avoid foods that cause inflammation, including processed foods, wheat, sugar, genetically modified foods, and bad fats like fried foods, seed oils, and vegetable oils.

What we avoid eating is more important than what we actually eat.

Up to 60 percent of the human adult body is water. According to H.H. Mitchell's article in the *Journal of Biological Chemistry* (volume 158), the brain and heart are composed of 73 percent water, and the lungs are about 83 percent water. The skin contains 64 percent water. The muscles and kidneys are 79 percent, and even the bones are watery, at a whopping 31 percent.

Water in our bodies helps give cells their structure and keeps them plump. It also helps create the different chemical reactions cells need to do their jobs. Water is also in charge of moving things around the cell to keep it working.

When it comes to hydration, I primarily drink high-quality water, freshly made fruit or vegetable juices, and quality teas. I minimize alcohol consumption and avoid sodas, especially diet sodas, sports drinks, and prepackaged juices.

In recent years, sleep has emerged as a key pillar of mental and physical health, and many books have been written on this subject. Chronic insomnia is estimated to affect approximately 30 percent of the general population. A sound sleep routine is critical for entrepreneurial effectiveness and essential for cognitive and physical health. I generally get the recommended seven to eight hours of sleep every night.

According to the American Lung Association, asthma is the most common chronic condition among children, currently affecting an estimated six million children under the age of eighteen. What's causing these respiratory issues in our society, especially in children? I believe the answer to this lies in all the toxic elements we breathe daily, in and outside the home. Some things are odorless, while others have beautiful aromas, making them hard to detect as potential poisons.

After moving into our family home in 2012, Myriam and the kids seemed to be getting sick all the time. Myriam, who rarely had colds or the flu, developed pneumonia and was rushed to the ER twice that year. It was a nightmare.

Our holistic health instincts kicked into high gear again, and we wanted to get to the root of the problem. Myriam believed that something in the house was making them sick. After all, her symptoms felt relieved when she was outside and were triggered when she was in our home, and even worse when she was upstairs.

We hired an air quality consultant who quickly detected the issues. He checked the house for mold/mycotoxins, and it came up negative. However, we had toxic insulation in our attic that dated to the 1970s and even some pipes wrapped in asbestos, probably dating to the 1950s or 1960s. Our upstairs air-conditioning units were filled with dust and debris, and our old ducts were lined with fiberglass, which loosened and got into the air. That explained the yellow residue on our glass dining table!

We moved out for a month while a crew of specialists with full hazmat suits removed all the toxic insulation and asbestos from our attic, being extremely careful not to contaminate the rest of the house and the surrounding outside area. Another company replaced all our

AC units and the fiberglass ducts with stainless steel ones. Once we moved back into the house, Myriam and the kids no longer experienced any respiratory or health issues.

Standard cleaning products in the home are big offenders and yet are too easily ignored as significant sources of toxins in our air. Cleaning products are some of the most toxic consumer products, made with harsh, petroleum-based ingredients designed to strip dirt and grease. They are laced with lemon and flower aromas to make them pleasant, covering up the toxic truth they are hiding.

If respiratory problems are an issue for you or your loved ones, the chemicals or mold you breathe in your home or workplace is likely the root cause.

Being an entrepreneur can be very uncomfortable and can cause severe stress. Managing stress is a priority and one of the most essential pillars of health—the key to maintaining a clear, decisive mind. Techniques like meditation and simple physical activities help manage stress.

To reduce my stress, I exercise regularly. Any movements will do. Push-ups, jumping jacks, running, and even walking around the neighborhood can have a positive physiological impact.

In my late forties, like so many men, I started having lower back issues, which were the first real signs of aging I had ever felt. My orthopedic doctor told me to avoid performing high-impact activities like jogging, horseback riding, or jet skiing.

One day, after returning from a vacation where I loaded heavy suitcases and carried my kids through airports, my back hurt so much that it was difficult to get out of my car. I was about to turn fifty, but I felt eighty.

Coincidentally, I was introduced to a personal trainer who had just moved to Miami from Eastern Europe. He told me he could help me fix my back issues. He went on to explain that he had a significant back injury in his athletic career that he was able to heal without surgery or medication.

I hired him, and I felt a remarkable improvement in my mobility within a week. In ninety days, my back was 100 percent healed. I went on to train with him five days a week for three years. He encouraged me to run, something I had never done in my life and something my doctor discouraged. At first, I ran half a mile slowly twice a week. Eventually, I ramped it up to two nine-minute miles. I enjoyed running so much that it became an addiction. Between 2019 and 2020, I ran almost 1,000 miles in two-mile runs. That means I ran 250 times a year, reminding myself that consistency is a great weapon.

In February 2022, I ran the Miami Half-Marathon (13.1 miles) in two hours and forty-five minutes. It's not much, but it was my life's most outstanding athletic achievement. Unfortunately, pushing myself to train for and run the half-marathon hurt my back. I had to stop running for a year, but recently, I started again with one-mile runs once in a while. This was a great lesson that less is more. Taking smaller runs more often never hurt me, but long runs less often did me in.

A consistent, moderate exercise routine, rather than intense, sporadic workouts, has been vital to maintaining my physical health and agility. Many people push themselves in exercise intensity only to give up quickly from muscle pain or injury. I prefer consistency over intensity. Consistency develops habits; intensity can be increased once the habit is formed.

Like the body, it is important to keep the mind in good shape. In 1993, I began reading psychology books, and I even attended a couple of self-help seminars, which prompted immense emotional change for me around the age of twenty-four.

Like many entrepreneurs, selling my business was a difficult transition that exposed mental health issues. From one day to the next, I went from being the CEO of TAOS to being an at-home dad. I love being a dad, but the transition took work.

After selling the business, I beat myself up for failing to maximize my company's purchase price. Deep inside, I felt like it was my fault. Rationally, I understood the unforeseen financial crisis led to our company's value reduction. Don't get me wrong; I am very grateful for my outcome. These feelings were not rational or driven by greed. I knew I had done better than I could have imagined when I started years earlier. But I also knew I left a lot of money on the table, a hard pill to swallow.

Despite all the blessings I was experiencing, I still felt anxious and fearful about what the future had in store for me. That made me realize I needed to focus on my mental and physical well-being, which I had neglected in my thirties, like many hardworking entrepreneurs.

That prompted me, for the past fourteen years, to undergo therapy to improve my mental health.

Therapy enabled me to understand and deal with some traumas I had experienced in my youth that caused me to have fears, anxiety, and low self-worth. Low self-worth is not the same as low self-esteem, which are not mutually exclusive feelings. Self-esteem is how we value and perceive ourselves. We can have high self-esteem by feeling we are successful parents, spouses, business people, or athletes. Self-worth, on the other hand, is the feeling of being good enough and worthy of love.

Traumatic experiences are widespread in people's lives, some worse than others. The traumas I am referring to are relative to my life experiences. Traumas can affect us psychologically as well as physically, as they can impair our ability to reach our full potential in life and business and weaken our immune defenses.

As part of my therapies, I was introduced to techniques like hypnosis and eye movement desensitization and reprocessing (EMDR), which are brain hacks that can accelerate the healing of our emotional issues. Hypnosis and EMDR are the application of methods and technologies to affect an individual's mental state, cognitive processes, or level of function. The main difference between EMDR and hypnosis is how they approach traumatic memories as well as how they root out the underlying thought processes causing the posttraumatic stress disorder (PTSD) symptoms. The most obvious difference is the hypnotic state itself, as in EMDR the individual does not go into a trance-like state.

A year ago, I started practicing daily meditation, which has been scientifically proven to be an effective way to manage stress. This has done wonders for me in a short time frame. I follow a practice called transcendental meditation (TM), but any meditation will have a positive impact.

It is hard to measure how your emotional state will impact your business. However, the bigger picture for entrepreneurs is to be aware of their emotions, deal with stressful situations, communicate well with people, empathize with others, and manage conflicts effectively. Most importantly, entrepreneurs need to make good decisions at all times.

Investing in physical and mental well-being is one of the greatest business investments entrepreneurs can make, and should be a top priority. This can have a disproportionate impact on our ability to succeed in business and enjoy the fruits of our success as we age.

A natural lifestyle is a journey. I hope you will join us—in everything you do—as you pursue the path to optimal wellness.

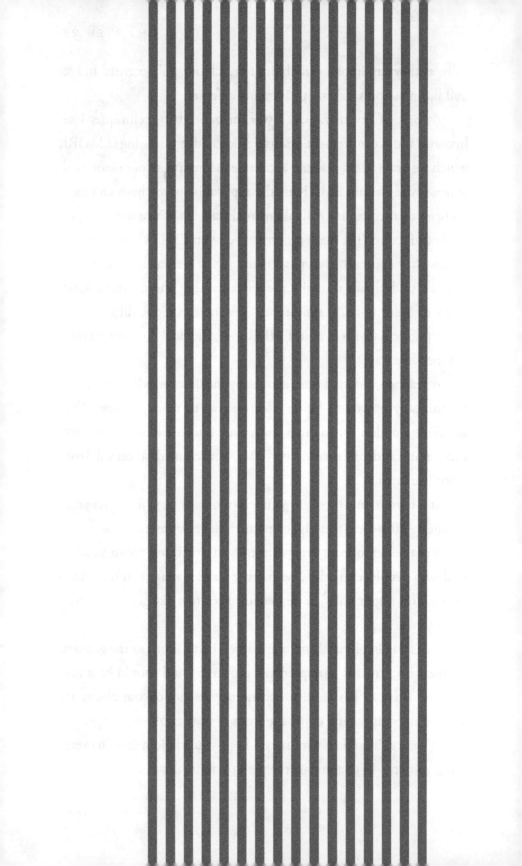

CONCLUSION

The most significant benefit of being an entrepreneur is that we can blur the lines between business, personal philosophy, and lifestyle. The more we discover our passions and purpose, the more we can infuse them into our work.

In my case, I was not particularly passionate about shaving. Like most men, I didn't enjoy it much, but shaving became a business opportunity. In spite of this, I became very passionate about TAOS business by infusing it with my life's passion and mission. Providing the perfect shave was what we sold, but our purpose was much deeper than that; it was about "helping men be healthier."

We took a shaving concept that had been around in Europe for a couple hundred years and made it relevant to modern American consumers. We can call these intangible elements the "magic" of TAOS brand.

We started by elevating the shaving category to an art form by introducing luxury and quality to our products and packaging.

We then incorporated plant-based ingredients into our formulas and removed harsh chemicals that are unhealthy to put on our skin.

We created a winning company culture of passionate employees who behaved like owners.

We became obsessively customer-focused.

We thrived on innovation to set our brand apart from all our competitors.

In turn, we became more passionate about how we did business than we were about the shaving category itself.

From the beginning, our customers regularly made comments like, "The last time I had a straight razor shave was on my wedding day," or "My dad used to take me with him to the barber." As a marketer, this is as strong an emotional connection as you can get for a consumer brand. We knew we had touched a chord with our customers but never knew how deep the relationship was, until we heard comments like these.

Before acquiring us, P&G ran a consumer survey on TAOS. They found our customer rating to be 84.6 out of 100. This was the highest customer rating they had ever seen. The next highest record was Gillette, which came in at around 75.

After the acquisition, they wanted to understand what made consumers obsessively loyal to the TAOS brand. They hired a consulting firm to investigate and report back on our brand's magic sauce.

Myriam and I instinctively thought that the magic sauce was in the superior efficacy and quality of our natural shaving products. However, to our amazement, P&G's research came up with something we didn't expect.

When interviewing loyal consumers, they noticed people rarely mentioned products or even the outstanding results they had when using them. That was a given. What they described was the experience of using the system. That time, each morning, they cared for themselves using special high-quality tools and products, following the 4 Elements of the Perfect Shave.

Digging further, the consultants concluded that we had tapped into a ritual, which they explained is the highest connection you can have with your consumer. This ritual was both primal and uniquely masculine. Shaving our faces is the one thing that only men do.

We had inadvertently captured a primitive male ritual that dates back to the cavemen era.

Myriam and I were fascinated with this revelation. P&G allowed us to reverse engineer the brand we had created in our twenties out of pure instinct. Looking under the hood of our brand was an incredible learning experience for us as marketers. While working inside P&G, they provided us with invaluable learning about their famous corporate disciplines, branding, and marketing expertise.

Steve Jobs is famous for being critical of market research. He once said: "It's tough to design products by focus groups. Often, people don't know what they want until you show it to them."

I completely agree with his philosophy, although our reason for not doing a focus group was a lack of resources. However, had we run a focus group before starting TAOS, consumers would have asked for shaving cream in a small plastic tube they could throw in a gym bag to shave at the gym after their workout. Instead, we went the complete opposite way by offering a four-step regimen with glass bottles, fancy razors, and shaving brushes at ten times the price.

Our lack of industry expertise allowed us to think outside the box without boundaries. If I had known then what I know now, I wouldn't have created TAOS the same way.

It is another reminder that a weakness can be a great strength.

Although I couldn't access company records, I kept tabs on TAOS's progress after leaving. At its peak, TAOS generated more than $100 million annually in revenue with 145 free-standing stores across the United States. I heard that P&G had invested substantially in the brand, but the company was operating with heavy losses.

From the outside, I could see signs the brand and the stores were losing their luster. Companies and brands often experience a business decline after a huge strategic buyer acquires them.

By 2019, I heard through the grapevine that P&G wanted to close most stores. During the pandemic, P&G closed all but two of its best stores and shifted its marketing efforts to online sales. I was recently informed that the last two stores will be closed in 2024. TAOS is now available online exclusively.

I am often asked if I am perturbed that TAOS was unsuccessful after its acquisition. Of course, I would have preferred to see TAOS remain a successful brand. Aside from our legacy, TAOS's success has directly impacted my reputation and personal street credit as an entrepreneur and now as an investor.

I am comforted that our little company pioneered a whole new industry catering to men's grooming. Almost everywhere I travel, I see that TAOS lives on in upscale barbershops cropping up worldwide. I can see TAOS's influence on many innovative men's grooming brands that cultivated from our pioneering efforts. Some of which we have invested in such as Barberino's, an Italian men's grooming brand with twenty barber shops in Italy and one in New York City.

While I am very passionate about the brand we created, it was just a means to an end for me to achieve financial freedom. If I had to do it all over again, I would do it almost the same way. My goal was to build and sell my business to have the freedom to design my life as I wanted, and that is precisely what I did.

Looking back on my journey, I reflect on how lucky I was over the years. I was lucky that my family moved to Montreal, Canada, bringing me closer to American culture. I was lucky to have met my incredible wife, Myriam, whose talents were instrumental to my success and our fate that brought us to NYC; nowhere else would our success story ever have been possible. We were so lucky for the *New York Times* article that propelled our company's sales, for Neiman Marcus executives to find us, for P&G to acquire Gillette, and for all the extraordinary people who helped us along the way.

Benjamin Franklin wisely said, "Don't put off until tomorrow what you can do today." How many of us speak about our goals and dreams in the future tense? The problem is that we think we have time.

Jesse Itzler, a serial entrepreneur and mentor, framed this concept well, and reminded me that the average person lives 28,500 days. Doing the quick math, I realized I had already used 20,000 to get here today. Realizing that I may only have 8,000 days left made me think about all the places I want to see, the goals I want to achieve, and the people I want to spend time with.

Life is short, so don't wait too long to go after what you want. Whatever that is for you.

In his book *Small Giants*, Bo Burlingham says, "Entrepreneurs are the artists of the business world." I couldn't agree more. I always saw the creativity in my work to paint a different future for my companies and bring those visions to life. Instead of brushes and paint, we use commerce to create businesses, ideas, products, services, opportunities, and business models. I applaud the innovative spirit of all entrepreneurs.

A frame in my office reads, "I am not delusional; I am an entrepreneur."

It's a reminder that if you shoot for the moon, even if you miss, you'll land among the stars.

ACKNOWLEDGMENTS

I want to acknowledge and thank all the people who had a positive impact on my life. A special acknowledgment to those who helped make this project a reality:

Myriam Malka: Thank you for being on this adventure with me for the past thirty years.

Dylan and Brandon: Thank you for being my teachers and my inspiration to tell our family's story.

Janette Barredo: Thank you for being such a great sounding board on this project and for all your support and encouragement.

My South Florida Entrepreneurs' Organization forum, including Ben, Gino, Jack, Jason, Jeff, Robert, and Ron: Thank you for all your support and love and for always having my back.

My EO forum, with Dan, David, Frido, Joel, Max, and Ron: Thank you for your support and for your contagious entrepreneurial spirit.

The Forbes Publishing team of Alison, Laura, Kristin, Nate, Heath, Analisa, Erin, and especially Kate: Thank you for your kindness and professionalism.

And P&G management: Thank you for your support in providing approval to use your trademarks and photography for this book.

ABOUT THE AUTHOR

Eric Malka, cofounder of The Art of Shaving and managing partner of Strategic Brand Investments, is a serial entrepreneur, investor, coach, author, and natural health advocate. Eric is credited for pioneering the luxury men's grooming and barbering industry.